Genesis thru Revelation: Complete Bible Study

Teacher's Copy

Second Edition

Ed Genske Ph.D.

WESTBOW
P R E S S®
A DIVISION OF THOMAS NELSON
& ZONDERVAN

The Guideposts Parallel Bible; Copyright; 1981; The Zondervan Corporation; Grand Rapids, Michigan.

Scripture taken from the Holy Bible, NEW INTERNATIONAL VERSION®. Copyright © 1973, 1978, 1984 by Biblica, Inc. All rights reserved worldwide. Used by permission. NEW INTERNATIONAL VERSION® and NIV® are registered trademarks of Biblica, Inc. Use of either trademark for the offering of goods or services requires the prior written consent of Biblica US, Inc.

This book is a work of non-fiction. Unless otherwise noted, the author and the publisher make no explicit guarantees as to the accuracy of the information contained in this book and in some cases, names of people and places have been altered to protect their privacy.

WestBow Press books may be ordered through booksellers or by contacting:

WestBow Press
A Division of Thomas Nelson & Zondervan
1663 Liberty Drive
Bloomington, IN 47403
www.westbowpress.com
1 (866) 928-1240

Because of the dynamic nature of the Internet, any web addresses or links contained in this book may have changed since publication and may no longer be valid. The views expressed in this work are solely those of the author and do not necessarily reflect the views of the publisher, and the publisher hereby disclaims any responsibility for them.

Any people depicted in stock imagery provided by Thinkstock are models, and such images are being used for illustrative purposes only. Certain stock imagery © Thinkstock.

ISBN: 978-1-5127-2532-2 (sc)
ISBN: 978-1-5127-2531-5 (e)

Library of Congress Control Number: 2015921383

Print information available on the last page.

WestBow Press rev. date: 02/11/2016

Contents

Preface

If you have never studied the Bible from cover to cover you are now in for the journey of a lifetime. No other book can tell you the things that the Bible tells you.

This second edition is done as a continuous improvement effort. Rewriting in some areas with refined editing is what has been done in this new edition. God's Word is the same yesterday, today, and forever. The goal here is to continuously improve the way the Word is taught for the student's benefit.

It is recorded in Acts 8:26-39 how Philip helped the Ethiopian man to understand the words of scripture he had been reading. Philip asked him if he understood what he was reading. The Ethiopian said "How can I unless someone explains it to me?" Philip went on to explain the Scriptures to him. The man believed and was baptized. The hearing of God's Word had its intended effect on that man long ago; and it does on you and me today.

"Genesis thru Revelation: Complete Bible Study" (was entitled: "Complete Bible Study: Genesis through Revelation") was written to accomplish three main goals. First and foremost was to provide another way to help people grow their faith in God and in his son Jesus. In this study you will see that the only way to gain everlasting life is through faith in him. How can people understand this if it is not explained to them? The better we understand God's Word the deeper will be our appreciation for the value of his Word as the authoritative source of truth in all matters of faith and life. When we treasure his Word we bring him glory. This is accomplished by providing every human being an easy to follow and easy to understand study of all 66 books of the Bible. By reviewing each of the books the student will come to realize the precious messages contained in it. Each book, each event, and each person encountered within its pages in some way reveals God's plan to redeem a fallen world. It is in that redemptive process that we grow in our faith, love, and service to him; and that brings glory to God.

A second reason to write this Bible study is because the need is there. I have taught many types of Bible study classes to fourth graders, high school students, and adults for over 40 years. A reoccurring issue I faced was that many of the students of all ages lacked a good basic knowledge of the whole Bible.

- How do the many people and events that are mentioned in the Bible all link together to form a complete single message for all of mankind for all of time?
- How did Abraham, Esther, Paul, Noah, Ruth, Peter, and many others impact the formation of the Christian church?

It is like painting a beautiful picture of a seascape. The artist paints all of the parts of the painting: the clouds, the sunset, the breakers crashing on the rocky shore, the rocky cliff, the colorful flowers, and the trees. It is when all of those parts are properly arranged on the canvas in their proper location do we see the resulting beautiful seascape picture. So it is with the Bible. This Bible study will help you put most of the main people and events in proper order so you will see the beautiful and essential message it is intended to give.

The way this material is written reveals the third main goal for writing it. This study can be used in a number of different venues. This book can be used in:

- Formal classroom settings for juniors or seniors in high school.
- Formal classroom settings for freshmen or sophomores in collage.
- Adult group Bible study.
- Individual Bible study.
- High school or adult Sunday school.

The way this is accomplished is by the teacher, instructor, or group leader varying the depth and scope of each session. The 32 sessions cover almost all of the main events and people in the Bible and can be completed in one typical school year.

Acknowledgements

To God be the glory for his guidance and direction.

To my wife, Kathy, and my daughter, Nikki, who have been supportive of this project from the beginning. Many hours were spent in writing and rewriting this material and a lot of that time was taken away from them.

To the adult Sunday school class at The Lutheran Church of the Messiah in Saginaw, Michigan. They went through prototype sessions of this book. Their suggestions and recommendations were important. Their testimonials provided needed encouragement.

About the Author

This brief overview of the author of "Genesis thru Revelation: Complete Bible Study" is intended to show that we can continue to grow in the knowledge of God's Word, no matter how much knowledge we have or experiences we have faced.

Ed Genske, the author who is now in his 60's as of this writing, has been a Christian his whole life thanks to the efforts of his God-fearing parents and by God's grace. Through his growing years he gained a deep love for God's Word. As a teenager in the 1960's he first taught the fourth grade Sunday school class at his church. Later he became the teacher for the high school class. In 1970 he completed a two-year train-the-teacher course in the "Bethel Bible Series" which was authored by Rev. Harley A. Swiggum. That course covered the entire Bible in two years of study. It was that course that planted the seed that eventually germinated into this Bible study. Since the 1970's Ed has lead Bible studies in both high school and adult settings, most of the time writing his own material.

As far as formal training and education is concerned Ed completed a patternmaking apprenticeship, obtained a bachelor's degree from Saginaw Valley State University, a master's degree from Central Michigan University, and a Ph.D. from Kennedy-Western University in business, with focus on management, finance, and organizational development.

Ed was employed as an engineer in the auto industry and recently retired having worked 48 years with his same employer. He also retired from his adjunct faculty position after 21 years from Saginaw Valley State University. Now he has more time to do God's work.

Ed has held many positions of responsibility both inside and outside his church. He is currently in his eleventh year as President of his local church, a position he has also held in two other churches as well. He has also worked on many other boards and committees in the management of the church.

Ed believes in Jesus Christ as his Lord and Savior. He also believes that the 66 books of the Bible are God's inerrant Word. His Christian teachings over four decades have demonstrated and witnessed to that fact. This book also demonstrates that fact.

Introduction

Topics from the entire Bible have been grouped into 32 sessions that can be studied in either a formal or informal setting. Each session covers main events and/or people relevant to the Bible's main message. The main message is that God's plan to save a fallen world was accomplished through the redemptive act of his son, Jesus, who died on the cross. For all who believe in Jesus he will grant eternal life. By the time you complete all 32 sessions you will have spent some time in every one of the 66 books in the Bible.

A feature called "Progress" is located at the end of each session. It looks like the following line of letters and numbers. Each letter and/or number represents the first letter of each of the 66 books, i.e., "G" for Genesis and so forth. As you proceed through this study you will see increasingly more of the letters and numbers highlighted to indicate your progress through the entire Bible.

GELNDJJR1S2S1K2K1C2CENEJPPESIJLEDHJAOJMNHZHZM–MMLJAR1C2CGEPC1T2T1T2TTPHJ1P2P1J2J3JJR

Getting started with anything worthwhile in life means making a commitment to do the things necessary to complete the endeavor. In this case a personal commitment of time is essential. If you are successful in keeping this time commitment you will never view the Bible the same way. The main events and personalities of the Bible will fall into place enabling you to understand more fully its main message.

The answers to the questions and the notes you take in each session should be saved and used in other Bible studies. This course will provide you with a good foundation upon which you can build a greater knowledge of the Word. The more time you spend in God's Word the deeper your faith will grow. Pray that God will lead you and empower you in your studies.

References

There can be no doubt that without good sound references a book like this one cannot be accomplished in a proper manner. Every effort has been taken to ask pertinent questions and in the "Teacher Copy" to provide the answers. Throughout this writing the goal has been to achieve 100% accuracy. It is my ongoing prayer that God will lead all of us to completion of that goal. The main references used while writing this book are as follows.

1. The Holy Bible, New International Version ®; Copyright© 1984 by International Bible Society.
2. The Guideposts Parallel Bible; Copyright © 1981; The Zondervan Corporation; Grand Rapids, Michigan.
3. Luther's Small Catechism; Copyright © 1986; Concordia Publishing House; St. Louis, Missouri.
4. Who's Who in the Bible; Copyright © 1994; The Reader's Digest Association, Inc.; New York, New York.
5. Atlas of the Bible; Copyright © 1981; The Reader's Digest Association, Inc.; New York, New York.
6. Halley's Bible Handbook; Copyright © 1965; The Zondervan Publishing House; Grand Rapids Michigan.
7. Concordia Self-Study Commentary; Copyright © 1979; Concordia Publishing House; St. Louis, Missouri.
8. What the Bible Is All About; Henrietta C. Mears; Copyright 1966; Regal Books Division, Gospel Light Publications; Glendale, California.

Designing Your Course

"Genesis thru Revelation: Complete Bible Study" has been designed to be flexible enough to be a great learning experience, particularly to the following groups of people:

- High school aged:
  - Text book for junior or senior courses
  - Bible study groups
  - Sunday school
  - Individual Bible study
- College age students:
  - Text book for freshman or sophomore courses
  - Bible study groups
  - Sunday school
  - Individual Bible study
- Adults:
  - Bible study groups
  - Sunday school
  - Individual Bible study

This study material is designed so that every student has their own "Student's Copy". The course teacher simply needs to design the course requirements appropriate for the type of class that is planned. This is done by varying course requirements and adjusting the depth and breadth of topics covered. For example the teacher can pick the level of requirements appropriate for the intended group, such as:

- Level 1 – Read the Bible passages and answer the questions together in class. This is appropriate for high school and adult Sunday school, Bible study groups, or individual Bible study. Level 1 requirements will take about an hour to cover in class and requires no homework in preparation for class.

- Level 2 – In addition to Level 1 activity above answer the "Discussion Questions" found near the end of each session. This is appropriate for high school and adult Sunday school, Bible study groups, or individual Bible study. Level 2 requirements will take about an hour and a half to cover in class and requires no homework in preparation for class.

- Level 3 – In addition to Levels 1 and 2 activities above review or read selected portions of the "Suggested Readings" found at the end of each session. Level 3 requirements are recommended for more formal classroom instruction for high school level courses or for advanced adult Bible study. It will take about two hours or more to cover in class and requires homework in preparation for class.

- <u>Level 4</u> – In addition to levels 1 through 3 activities above read assigned portions of the "Suggested Readings" found at the end of each session. This level of requirements is recommended for formal college freshman or sophomore classroom instruction, or for advanced adult Bible study. It will take about two hours or more to cover in class and requires homework in preparation for class.

Regardless of which level is planned, the teacher's job is the same:

- Pray in every class session that the Holy Spirit will guide the students and teacher to a greater understanding of God's Word.
- Design the course work appropriate for the students you will be leading.
- Motivate the students to attend and participate in class work and discussions.
- Be prepared for each class. This is an important task and should not be taken lightly.
- Use wall maps to add geographical insights into discussions.
- Start all classes on time.
- Keep the discussions focused so that the course can end on time.
- Give God the glory for great things he will accomplish in your class.

May God bless your efforts!

Creation – Session 1

Opening Prayer

Lord God you are the Creator of all. May your Holy Spirit guide us in this study of your Word so that we accurately learn your true message. Bless us with the time and patience to not only begin this study; but that we can complete it through to the end. In this effort we seek to grow our faith and give glory you. In Jesus's name we pray. Amen

Introduction

The goal of this first lesson is to study the Bible's account of how God created the world and all that is in it. The beginning of everything (except God because he has always existed) is where the first verse of the first page of the first book of the Bible begins. It is good to begin with the real beginning so that a solid foundation can be established for the study of the rest of the Bible.

Session Material

1. It is fitting that we understand how it all got started so we can more fully understand the Bible's main message, i.e., that we have a loving God who provides a way for us to spend eternity with him even though we do not always deserve it. Read Genesis 1:1 and fill in the following blanks: "In the _____ _____ _____ the heavens and earth". Deeply pondering these words enriches our understanding of the Bible's account of creation. God, not some random chance event, has made us who we are.

2. The word "genesis" means beginning, the origin, or the coming into being of something. Everything had a beginning except God. What does Revelation 1:8 say about God? He is the _____ and the _____. This means God is the beginning and the end of all of his creation. He reigns over all of creation then, now and forever.

3. Let's get to know God a little better. Based on the following Bible passages briefly describe many of his admirable characteristics. (Continued on the next page.)

Passages	Characteristics of God
John 4:24	
1 Timothy 1:17	
James 1:17	
Genesis 17:1 & Matthew 19:26	
John 21:17	

Jeremiah 23:23-24	
Leviticus 19:2	
Deuteronomy 32:3-4	
2 Timothy 2:13	
Psalm 145:9	
Jeremiah 3:12	
Exodus 34:6-7	
Exodus 3:14	

4. The Bible assumes and nowhere questions the fact that God has always existed and is always within reach of each one of us. He is just one prayer away. Another fact about God is that He is a Triune God meaning three persons in one; those being God the _____, God the _____, and God the _____.

Note: You might wonder how God could be three persons in one. Our limited minds have a hard time understanding this concept this side of the grave. But, consider H_2O, the chemical symbol for water. It can be a liquid. Freeze water and you get a solid. When you heat up water you get a gas or steam. Thus we can see water in three different states. Nothing is impossible for God.

5. "In the beginning God created the heavens and earth." What does the term "created" mean in this context? Consider this. In Genesis 1:2 we see that before the "beginning" the earth was_____, _____, and _____. God had few resources to work with, but he had the most important resource, that being his almighty power. As he spoke, it came into being. A painter "creates" a beautiful painting. But, he or she has a canvas, paint, a paint brush, and an imagination with which to work. When God created He made everything out of _____. Therefore, all of creation is directly linked to the real Creator, God Almighty.

6. (A) God created everything in six days and rested on the seventh day. Read Genesis 1 and according to the following verses record what our God created in each of the first six days.

Day	Verses	What Was Created?
1	3-5	
2	6-8	
3	9-13	
4	14-19	
5	20-23	
6	24-31	

(B) Did God really create everything in six days? Yes! Notice in verses 5, 8, 13, 19, 23, and 31 of Genesis 1 that it says:"And there was evening, and there was morning....." We can count the days as we read through Genesis 1. Also, in Exodus 20:11 note that it actually mentions that God created it all in six days. God created everything very good except one thing. Note in Genesis 2:18 that God said it is not good for _____. So God made him a suitable helper. God made Eve and together they were able to reproduce and realize life as God had intended it to be.

7. God gave man roles and responsibilities. Note what the following passages say that man was created to do while here on earth.

Passages	Roles and Responsibilities
Psalm 8:6-8	
Genesis 1:28a	
Genesis 1:28b	
Genesis 2:15	

Note: Our Creator created a world that would meet the needs of his children. He gave man a special place to live. Can you imagine a world in perfect harmony in every way?

8. God did not create the world and walk away. He is deeply involved in it and in us every day. God remains closely bonded to it and to us. Read Psalm 121:1-8 to see how.

Verses	What Does God Do for Us?
3	
7	

9. Man is not an accident or a creature of evolutionary chance. All, even man, was put into place by our creator. Even though God wants man to be the ruler and caretaker of his creation, who ultimately owns and controls everything according to 1 Chronicles 29:10-14 and Psalm 24:1-2? _____

_____

10. God has given man freedom (a free will) to do what he wants, but within limits. We are to live within God's laws of thou shall and thou shall not do certain things. What happens to those who choose to live outside of God's rules according to Hebrews 11:6? _____

_____

11. Because God loves us he gives us guidelines to live by. The Law (the Ten Commandments and the Old Testament) and the Gospel are given so that we can learn how to live a life that is pleasing to him. Since we cannot keep all of the law

what does the Gospel teaches us according to 1 John 1:9? _____

_____

_____

12. Read Genesis 1:26-27.
(A) In whose image did God created man? _____

(B) Why?_____

_____

Note: Man was created to be the crown of his creation. God wanted a creature in his own image to have fellowship with him. Also God wanted man to manage his magnificent earth. God gave man special characteristics:

- Rational – We can think through problems and situations.
- Conscience – We are able to discern what is right and what is wrong.
- Emotional – We can be happy or sad and we can give and receive love.
- Mind – We are able to learn and remember facts, figures, and information.
- Soul – We will someday die but a part of us (our soul) will go on living with God forever if we believe in him.

Note: God created everything in six days and his creation was very good. On the seventh day God rested from all of his work. To believe in a six-day creation as recorded in the Bible is no harder to believe than the man-made theories describing how the universe evolved over billions of years. Scientists make assumptions and then based on those assumptions develop theories about the formation of the earth, the universe, man, and many other things. As new knowledge is learned assumptions and theories change. God's Word never changes. Why won't these scientists start with Biblical precepts and do their studies? We will discuss more later on about the "one" who is out there who wants to undermine God and draw people away from the truth.

Session 1 Discussion Questions

1. Given the long list of characteristics of God, why don't Christians want to get to know him better?

2. Given the long list of characteristics of God, why won't don't all people want to get to know him better?

3. Have I made God a priority in my life? If not how can I do it?

Suggested Reading for Session 2

Genesis 1 through 3

Progress:

GELNDJJR1S2S1K2K1C2CENEJPPESIJLEDHJAOJMNHZHZM–MMLJAR1C2CGEPC1T2T1T2TTPHJ1P2P1J2J3JJR

Paradise Is Lost - Session 2

Opening Prayer

Lord God long ago sin separated us from you. But, in your loving mercy you provided a path of salvation for all who believe through the redemptive act of your Son, Jesus. Guide our thinking and speaking so that we accurately reflect your written Word. Help us to internalize your Word and enrich our lives so that we are living a life worthy of your Son's sacrifice. In Jesus's name we pray. Amen

Introduction

In the last session we studied the actual and real account of how God created all things and how everything was very good. In this session we will study how God's created paradise was lost due to sin. We will also review the different writing styles found in the Bible.

Session Material

1. Man was honored by God by making him the most important part of His creation. God gave man three key roles according to Genesis 1:28. The first of those roles was to _____ the earth. Secondly, to have mankind _____ the earth; in other words to bring the earth under control. Man was to be the earth's caretaker. The third role for mankind was to be the _____ of the earth. In this role mankind is responsible to exercise power and authority over creation for its effective governance and management.

2. Let's visit the world's most beautiful garden. According to Genesis 2:4-15, we are given a vision of perfection where everything was living in _____ and _____. Man was created and was meant to live in harmony with _____, _____, _____ , and _____. Originally there were no barriers, strife, differences, nor were there any conflicts between Adam, Eve and God. We will see how sin changed all of that.

3. Will there ever be perfect tranquility and harmony again? _____ .To help you answer the question read Isaiah 65:17-25. This passage gives us a glimpse of what spending eternity with God will be like.

4. But, tranquility and harmony was conditional on man obeying God.
(A) Adam and Eve were told by God not to do something according to Genesis 2:16-17. What was it? _____

(B) By doing what they were not suppose to do, Adam and Eve were really seeking to become independent of God by making themselves judges of what is good and evil. That is something that is God's right to do alone. This was a test of _____. Eating from that tree meant disobeying God and they were making themselves to be their own god. At the very heart of sin is that we ignore God. Obedience was the ticket then and still is today. God commanded it then and still expects obedience today.

5. In Genesis 1:27-28 we notice that God created "male and female". In Genesis 2:18-24 we see that this is presented a second time in order to provide _____ _____ about the crown of his creation, man and woman. In addition, verse 24 elaborates on the _____ between a man and his wife. It is an inseparable union instituted by God. Divorce was not part of God's plan. God's plan was/is for a man and a woman only. See Genesis 2:24.

6. In Genesis 2:10-14 we are given clues as to the location of the Garden of Eden. Most experts believe the garden's location was in Southwestern Asia. Today the two rivers mentioned in verse 14, the _____ and the _____, flow today through the country of _____. Archeologists have unearthed very old civilizations along those rivers. Note the locations of these two rivers on a map.

7. (A) Tranquility and harmony did not last. Based on Genesis 3:1-14 what was the reason? _____

_____

(B) According to 2 Corinthians 11:3 & 14 who spoke to Eve through the serpent? _____ Sin entered into God's creation through one man; so it will be one man, Jesus, who will put an end to sin once and for all someday when he returns.

Note: The evil serpent used clever logic to persuade Eve into disobeying God. That same serpent uses clever logic and tactics to draw us away from God too. We need to be aware that the deceiver is active today. This is why we need to study and know God's Word, i.e., to help us avoid the evil one's cunning tactics.

8. Based on the following verses from Genesis 3 summarize God's responses to Adam and Eve's act of disobedience. (Continued on the next page.)

Verses	God's Responses
14	
15	
16	

17	
18	
19	

9. It was clear that sin separated Adam and Eve from God. According to the following verses from Genesis 3 note the evidence of that separation.

Verses	God's Responses
8	
10	
12	
13	

Note: So, guilt, fear and blame were their best defense for their sin. Perfect tranquility and harmony were lost. We live in this sin-filled world now but we will see conditions like those in the Garden of Eden again. One day when Jesus returns God will create a new heaven and earth. Like the Garden of Eden man will be brought back into perfect harmony with all things, especially with God. We will discuss this topic more fully in a later chapter.

10. Based on the following passages note the immediate and long term effects of original sin.

Passages	Effects
Genesis 3:23	
Romans 6:23a	

Note: Because of this original sin mankind lost the perfection God had intended for them. Everything had been in perfect harmony. Because of that sin, death crept into God's perfect creation. Mankind was cursed with hard work and then death.

11. But all hope is not lost. Genesis 3:15 and Romans 16:20 indicate that God has a plan to _____ _____ once and for all time. For the faithful in Christ, we will someday see the new heaven and earth when Jesus returns. At that time of the great and final judgment, God will cast all who are evil into the "lake of fire". All believers will spend eternity with God in a recreated earth which will be in perfect harmony in all ways. Tranquility will be restored.

12. How will that hope for a complete new beginning happen? Read John 3:16 and 14:6 and explain God's plan of salvation for mankind. _____

_____

_____

Note: Adam and Eve's experience with sin is not much different from what we face today. The devil and his angels are out there, roaming the around the earth seeking out people that can be deceived and tempted like Eve had been. We need to be ever vigilant and on guard to resist daily temptations.

Note: The origin of evil, how it got started, was from Lucifer, the devil himself who was a fallen angel. He coveted power and wanted to be a god. This occurred sometime after creation but before the Garden of Eden incident. God ejected him from heaven and down to the earth where he and his angels still exist today. (For additional study on this topic read Ezekiel 28, Isaiah 14, Job 1, and Matthew 4.)

13. Before we get too far along in this Bible study you may have already noticed different literary styles are used to present its message. Understanding this fact will help in understanding of God's Word. Note some of the following literary styles and examples in the following table. Note that there are many writing styles but still one main message about Jesus.

Literary Style	Examples
Hymns/Songs	Genesis 1:1-2:3, Judges 5:1-31, Luke 1:46-56 and Exodus 15:1-21
History	Luke 2:1-7 and Exodus 13 & 14
Poetry	Judges 15:15b-18 and most of Psalms
Figurative	Isaiah 55:12b
Fables	Judges 9:7-15
Metaphor	Psalm 80:8-12
Allegory	Ecclesiastes 12:2-5

Session 2 Discussion Questions

1. How do we seek independence from God like Adam and Eve?

2. What is God's will for my life?

3. When have you ever felt separated from God?

4. Was Adam and Eve's experience with sin any different from what we experience today?

Suggested Reading for Session 3

Genesis 4 through 11

Progress:

GELNDJJR1S2S1K2K1C2CENEJPPESIJLEDHJAOJMNHZHZM—MMLJAR1C2CGEPC1T2T1T2TTPHJ1P2P1J2J3JJR

Population Grows – Session 3

Opening Prayer

Lord God you are a loving God who created all things and sustains all things. You forgive all of our sins if we remain faithful. We know that one of the ways we can remain faithful to you is through the study of your Word. We ask that the Holy Spirit will continue to bless us with the insights we need to more fully understand you and your Word. Help us keep the study of your Word a priority in our lives. In Jesus's name we pray. Amen.

Introduction

In the last session we saw how sin separated man from God. Everything God had made was perfect and he ushered man into a perfect paradise. But, that paradise was lost because of sin. Adam and Eve were disobedient to God. In this session we will look into the period following the Eden events and how as the population grew so did sin.

Session Material

1. Sometime after the events in the Garden of Eden and as recorded in Genesis 4:1-2, what two events occurred which are the first and second of their kind in all of recorded history? _____

_____

2. Based on the following verses from Genesis 4 what other major events occurred?

Verses	Major Events
8-9	
10-12	
16	
17	

3. But where did Cain's wife come from? Read Genesis 4:18-22. _____

_____

Note: Adam and Eve's family tree grew over the centuries that they lived. In Genesis 3:20 it mentions that Eve was the mother of all living. All people are descendants of Adam and Eve. Later we will read about how long people lived and the fact that they had children over many generations.

4. According to Genesis 4:19 what was the second major sin recorded in all of history? _____

Note: God intended one man and one woman relationships when he instituted marriage and the family (Genesis 2:24).

5. In the typical world history class in school three major periods of time are studied. Write in each of the following approximate time periods that corresponds with its correct description.
Three time periods: Bronze Age, Iron Age, and Stone Age

Time Period	Description of the Time Periods
	A period of time before 2500 BC when man used crude tools.
	A period of time between 2500 BC and 1200 BC when man first started using metal tools.
	A period of time after 1200 BC when man smelted iron to make tools and weapons.

6. How do the activities found in the following verses from Genesis 4 seem to fit these time periods?

Verses	Activities
20	
21	
22	

7. Why was Seth, Eve's third recorded son, such a comfort to her and eventually to all who believe in God throughout all of history? See Genesis 4:25 and Luke 3:23 & 38.

To Eve	
To all believers	

8. Genesis 5 records some of Adam and Eve's descendants and how long they lived. According to Genesis 5:27 who lived to be the oldest person in recorded history and how long did he live? _____

Note: It is easy to understand how the world's population grew so fast. People lived a very long time continued to have children.

9. As time passed the population grew and so did sin. From the following verses in Genesis 6 describe the moral conditions at the time.

Verses	Moral Conditions
5	
11-12	

10. Based on Genesis 6:6 how did God feel about the conditions on earth at that time? _____

11. Based on Genesis 6:9-22 briefly describe what God's plan was to deal with sinful mankind? _____

_____

_____

12. Note what event Peter wrote about in 2 Peter 3:6 some 4000 years later?

_____

13. Genesis 7 and 8 record the events of the flood. Chapters 9 and 10 record events following the flood; and some of the movements of Noah's three sons. Based on the names that are recorded, historians have been able to trace the movements of Noah's sons and their families. According to the following verses from chapter 10 describe where each son went to begin new lives. Point the locations out on a map.

Verses	Son	Destination
2-4	Japheth	
6-20	Ham	
21-31	Shem	

14. List the four reoccurring ways people were organized as mentioned in Genesis 10:4, 20, 31 and, 32.

1.	3.
2.	4.

15. Sometime after the flood when there was still a common language among all people on earth. An incident occurred that angered God. Based on Genesis 11:1-9 answer the following questions? (Continued on the next page.)

Question	Verse	Answer
What incident is described?	9	
What did the people want to do?	4	

Why did God disapprove?	6	
What did God do?	9	

Session 3 Discussion Questions

1. Think back about your own family ancestors and if they had lived 800 or 900 years how big would your living family tree be today?

2. How far back can you trace your family tree?

3. Why do we not live to be hundreds of years old today? (See Romans 8:22)

Suggested Reading for Session 4

Genesis 12 through 22

Progress:

GELNDJJR1S2S1K2K1C2CENEJPPESIJLEDHJAOJMNHZHZM—MMLJAR1C2CGEPC1T2T1T2TTPHJ1P2P1J2J3JJR

The Covenant – Session 4

Opening Prayer

Lord God as we study your Word we ask that the Holy Spirit continue to instill an ever increasing willingness to see this study through to the end. The more we know about your Word the more effective witnesses we will be. May the words we say, the meditations of our heart, and the knowledge we learn enrich our lives and bring you glory. In Jesus's name we pray. Amen.

Introduction

In the last chapter we studied how the population grew over time, beginning with Adam and Eve. We saw how greed and envy resulted in Abel's death; how lust resulted in polygamy; and how pride and rebellion caused God to scatter people across the globe and confuse their language. In this session we go through more generations of people with our focus still on the family blood line that produced our Savior.

Session Material

1. Even though mankind was sinful God still had a purpose and a plan for them. He wanted a people that would ultimately be His chosen people who would:

(A) _____ to all nations and all people throughout the ages.

(B) _____ all of history from the first created people, Adam and Eve to our Savior, Jesus Christ. They would prepare the way for his first and second coming.

(C) _____ His Word, the Scriptures, throughout all time until Jesus returns.

(D) Remain _____ and _____ him.

2. Read Luke 3:36-38. After Noah, who would be the next person in Mary's (the mother of Jesus) bloodline? _____

3. In Genesis 12 we find the key event that helps us understand the main message of the Bible. Abram (Later called Abraham) would be the first chosen leader of God's chosen people, a people whose major task would be a beacon to the lost peoples of the world. This is the beginning upon which Israel's history would be built. Read Genesis 12:1-3 and notice that this is God's first covenant with what would become his chosen people.

(A) What is a covenant? _____
_____

(B) Fill in the missing words to the seven parts of God's covenant with Abram.

    (1) I will make you a great _____ ;

    (2) I will _____ you;

(3) I will make your _____ great;

(4) You will be a _____ to others;

(5) I will bless those who _____ you;

(6) I will curse those who _____ you;

(7) All peoples on earth will be _____ through you.

(C) These are the things God said he would do. What was Abram's responsibility?

_____

Note: Here God promises many great things to Abram. God placed in Abraham's hands the responsibility to follow his lead and put into motion events that would forge a course for a chosen people on into the future. All God asked is that they remain faithful to him. This event occurred about 2100 B.C.

Note: Abram was faithful but not perfect. You will notice other leaders that we will study later on in this course were not be perfect either. Leaders like Saul, David, Solomon, Peter, and Paul just to name a few. Perfection is not a prerequisite for God's calling. Throughout history God has and still does use imperfect people to carry out his perfect will. All of the faithful (us too) are called by God to use their four T's for his service: time, talents, treasures, and tithes.

4. Based on the following passages from Genesis briefly answer the questions about Abram as he begins his life's work.

Questions	Passages	Facts about Abram
Where was Abram from?	11:31	
What did God tell Abram to do?	12:1	
Who went with Abram?	12:4-5a	
To where did God lead him?	12:5b-6	
What did God promise to give to his offspring?	12:7a	
How did Abraham respond to God?	12:7b	

5. As time went on God expanded the covenant he had made with Abram and his descendants. The original covenant was detailed in question 3 above. Based on the following passages from Genesis, note the expanded covenant details. (Continued on the next page)

Passages	Added Covenant Details
12:7	
15:5	
17:5	
17:6	
17:7	
17:8	
28:14a	
28:14b	
28:15	

6. Based on the following passages from Genesis what was a major concern for Abram and what was God's response?

Passages	Concern and Outcome
15:2-3	
15:4-5	
21:1-3	

7. In Genesis 17:5 & 15 whose names were changed and what were they changed to:

Changed from:	Changed to:
Abram	
Sarai	

8. (A) Based on Genesis 21:4 what did Abraham do to his eight-day old son and why?

What: _____

Why: _____

(B) Read Genesis 17:9-14. What was the purpose of this act?

_____

_____

9. The following chapters from Genesis listed below covers some of the other events worth reading about in a more in-depth study of this book. These chapters complement the major events and people we have been studying. (Continued on the next page.)

Chapters	Events and People
13	Abram and Lot go their own ways
14	Lot is rescued by Abram – the first war
16	Hagar bears Abram's first son, Ishmael, Islam's first leader.
18	Abram pleads for Sodom
19	God destroys Sodom and Gomorrah
22	God orders Abraham to sacrifice Isaac

Session 4 Discussion Questions

1. The four T's of stewardship are: time, talents, treasures, and tithes. How do we know we are meeting God's stewardship expectations?

2. By God's grace through faith alone are we saved according to Ephesians 2:8-10. So where do our works come into play with respect to this passage?

3. Read James 2:17-18 and note how it explains faith and works.

4. Why do you think Canaan was the chosen location for the Promised Land?

Suggested Reading for Session 5

Genesis 22 through 35

Progress:

GELNDJJR1S2S1K2K1C2CENEJPPESIJLEDHJAOJMNHZHZM−MMLJAR1C2CGEPC1T2T1T2TTPHJ1P2P1J2J3JJR

The Covenant Renewed – Session 5

Opening Prayer

Lord God we ask that you be with us as we continue the study of your Word. We ask that your Holy Spirit engage us so that we can learn about the vitally important events and people that have shaped our history. Keep distractions away so we can focus on the important messages we need to learn. In Jesus's name we pray. Amen

Introduction

In the last session we studied about some of Noah's descendants who were to become Jesus' ancestors. We saw that God made a covenant with the patriarch, Abram. The covenant was a promise from God to build a people into a great nation so that they would be a blessing to the whole world. In this session we will study how God passed the covenant on to other generations. Our focus is still on the blood line that produced our Lord and Savior, Jesus Christ.

Session Material

1. God reaffirmed the covenant with Abraham five times, then to Isaac, and then to other leaders. God promised that the land of Canaan would be theirs forever. According to Genesis 22:17b what new information is given about Canaan, the Promised land? _____

_____

Note: The Promised Land was not just sitting there idle waiting for God's people to show up and claim it. Other people were already living there.

2. (A) Who were the Canaanites according to Genesis 10:6 & 15-19? _____

_____

(B) How would you describe these people according to Deuteronomy 7:1-7?

_____

Note: Archaeologists have excavated several sites and their findings have been appalling. Grossly immoral worship practices, worship to pagan gods, and child sacrifice were widely practiced by the Canaanites. Because of their awful sins note that in Deuteronomy 7:2 God tells his people to "destroy them totally".

3. God wanted his people to be special and avoid any influence from the pagan peoples around them. Describe how God intended his people to be separated from others three ways (Continued on the next page.):
(A) Geographically: _____
(B) Ethnically: _____

(C) Religiously: _____

(D) How does Genesis 24:1-4 provide an example of the ethnic separation God wanted for his people?_____

_____

4. Isaac married Rebekah, a woman from his father's (Abraham) country and relatives. Some years later they had twins. Based on the following passages from Genesis, answer the following questions about the twins.

Passages	Questions	Answers
25:21-26	What were they named?	
	Who was born first?	
25:29-34	How did Jacob get the birthright away from his brother?	
27:1-4	What did Isaac want Esau to do and why?	
27:33-35	Who received the family blessing and why?	
27:41	What was Esau's response to Jacob's deception?	
27:43-45	What did Jacob do as a result?	

5. (A) What was Isaac's command to Jacob based on Genesis 28:1-2? _____

_____

(B) According to Genesis 28:8-9 what did Esau do? _____

_____

6. According to the following verses from Genesis 28 answer the questions about Jacob's awesome experience on his way to his family's homeland. (Continued on the next page.)

Verses	Questions	Answers
10-12	What happened to Jacob and what did he see?	
13a	Who stood at the top of the stairway?	

13b-15	What was spoken to Jacob?	
16-19	What was Jacob's response to this experience?	
20-22	What did Jacob vow to God?	

7. Jacob had deceived his father and his brother in order to receive the family blessing. Read Genesis 29:13-30 and briefly describe how Isaac was deceived.

_____

_____

_____

8. As the years passed Jacob was blessed with many children. These children would form what would be known as the 12 tribes of Israel. Each tribe would be named after a son or grandson. God's promise of a great nation continued to develop. Based on the following passages, write in the names of Jacob's children. Note that there were four mothers involved. Also note that they were all boys except for one girl.

Number	Passages	Mothers	Children's Names
1	Genesis 29:32	Leah	
2	Genesis 29:33	Leah	
3	Genesis 29:34	Leah	
4	Genesis 29:35	Leah	
5	Genesis 30: 17-18	Leah	
6	Genesis 30:19-20	Leah	
7	Genesis 30:21	Leah	
8	Genesis 30:4-6	Bilhah	
9	Genesis 30:7-8	Bilhah	
10	Genesis 30:9-11	Zilpah	
11	Genesis 30: 12-13	Zilpah	
12	Genesis 30:22	Rachel	
13	Genesis 35:18	Rachel	

9. Based on Genesis 35:10 what was Jacob's name changed to? _____

10. The following passages record other key events worth reading about to get a fuller grasp of conditions in about 1900 B.C.

Passages	Events
Genesis 24	How Isaac finds Rebekah
Genesis 25	Ishmael's 12 sons – Arab names
Genesis 29	Jacob marries the wrong woman
Genesis 30-31	Jacob's dispute with his father-in-law
Genesis 32	Jacob wrestles with God
Genesis 33	Jacob reunites with Esau
Genesis 34	Dinah defiled – brothers get revenge

Session 5 Discussion Questions

1. The Canaanites worshiped pagan gods. One of their rituals was to sacrifice one of their children in order to bring good luck. What god is worshiped when a baby is sacrificed (aborted)?

2. As part of God's covenant with Abraham, Isaac, and Jacob the Promised Land would be theirs forever. Do you think the covenant is thought to be still in effect today in the minds of many Israelite people?

3. Question 3 above references the separation God wanted for his chosen people. Do we, the faithful, still need to be separated?

Suggested Reading for Session 6
Genesis 36 through 50

Progress:

GELNDJJR1S2S1K2K1C2CENEJPPESIJLEDHJAOJMNHZHZM–MMLJAR1C2CGEPC1T2T1T2TTPHJ1P2P1J2J3JJR

A Remnant Remains – Session 6

Opening Prayer

Lord God we do not deserve your grace. We sin daily and because of that our prayer is that you forgive us daily. Bless us with your forgiveness. Also continue to bless us with the time and energy to continue with this study of your Word. Please show us your ways and teach us your paths. In Jesus's name we pray. Amen

Introduction

In the last session we saw how the covenant, God's promise to his chosen people, was extended from Abraham's son Isaac and then to his grandson Jacob. We saw how Jacob deceived his father to get the family blessing. Then Jacob himself was deceived in his marriage to Leah. In this session we will study the events of Joseph's life in Egypt and how an evil act turned out to be a blessing to Jacob and his family.

Session Material

1. In the last session we reviewed the list of Jacob's children. How many were there? There were _____ brothers and _____ sister.

Note: So far we have seen how God has used imperfect people to fulfill his perfect plans. God uses both believers and non-believers to accomplish his will. In fact, God uses all of us in one way or another to fulfill his will. God can use evil to accomplish something good.

2. Jacob's second youngest son was Joseph. His mother was Rachel. That made him the favorite with Jacob. Remember, Jacob had to work 14 years to "earn" Rachel from her father so she could be his wife (Genesis 29). He loved her that much. Genesis 37 describes the events that led to Joseph being sold into slavery. What were some of the reasons why Joseph was sold into slavery based on the following verses from Genesis 37?

Verses	Reasons
3	
4	
5-8	
9-11	

3. To whom was Joseph sold according to the following verses from Genesis 37?

Verses	Who Bought Joseph?
25-28	
36	

4. According to the following verses from Genesis 39 what was Joseph's relationship with God while being Potiphar's slave?

Verses	Joseph's Relationship with God
2	
3-4	
5	

5. Read Genesis 39:6-20. Because Joseph resisted the advances of Potiphar's wife, he was falsely put into prison. But even in prison God's plan's for Joseph did not end. What happened based on the following verses from Genesis 39?

Verses	Joseph in Prison
21	
22	
23	

6. While in prison Joseph was blessed by God with the ability to interpret dreams. How did Joseph show his devotion to God according to Genesis 40:8? _____

_____

Note: Joseph showed how God was using him as an instrument of his will while imprisoned. Pharaoh had troubling dreams and he did not understand them. Word of Joseph's ability to interpret dreams reached Pharaoh so he summoned Joseph out of his jail cell.

7. Based on Genesis 41:25-30 what was Joseph's interpretation of Pharaoh's dreams?_____

_____

8. Pharaoh was pleased with the interpretations and as a result what did he do with Joseph according to Genesis 41:39-40. _____

_____

Note: Notice how God worked in Joseph's life; filled with ups and downs. Joseph was:
- A favored son.
- Sold as a slave.

- Made the head of an important official's house.
- Sent to prison based on false charges.
- Made the number two leader in Egypt, the most powerful nation of its day.

What a career path God had him experience, all in the span of 13 years. Without God's intervention into his life he probably would have lived the life of a farmer and shepherd in Canaan with his brothers. But, God had a plan and a purpose. The evil his brothers did to him turned out to be a blessing to their family.

9. What were Joseph's two sons named? (See Genesis 41:50-52.)
_____ and _____

10. Based on Genesis 41:53-57 how was the fulfillment of Pharaoh's dreams being carried out? _____
_____

Note: The famine was widespread, even in Canaan where Joseph's family still lived. They too needed to go to Egypt for food. One of the most touching stories you will ever read is captured in Genesis 42 through 46. In those pages of your Bible you will read about how revenge took a back seat to love and forgiveness. It records the events that lead up to Joseph's emotional reunion with his family. It is a lesson for us all and definitely worth a read!

11. Based on the following passages from Genesis how did Joseph react when he first saw his family?

Passages	Joseph's Reactions
43:30	
45:1-3	
45:14-15	
46:29	

Note: He held no animosity toward his brothers; only tears of joy and an attitude of forgiveness, hope and love.

12. Joseph had insight and was able to explain God's plan for his life. Note how God had blessed him with these insights which are found in the following verses in Genesis 45. (Continued on the next page.)

Verses	Joseph's Insights
4-7	
8	

9-11	

13. According to Genesis 47:27 where did Joseph have his family move to when they arrived in Egypt? _____

14. Jacob had taken his entire family to Egypt. Based on Genesis 46:26-27 how large was his family when this occurred? _____

15. In Genesis 48 and 49 Jacob pronounces blessings on all of his sons and on Joseph's two sons. Based on Genesis 49:8-10 and Luke 3:33 which son would continue the blood line of Mary, the mother of Jesus? _____

Session 6 Discussion Questions

1. How does God use believers and nonbelievers to accomplish his will?
   - Believers:

   - Nonbelievers:

2. How do the events of Joseph's enslavement and imprisonment teach us that when bad things happen to good people they need to realize God has a plan and a purpose?

3. Joseph held no animosity toward his brothers. He expressed tears of joy, forgiveness, hope and love. Is this a good example for us to follow when we are wronged by someone? Explain.

Suggested Reading for Session 7

Exodus 1 through 13

Progress:

GELNDJJR1S2S1K2K1C2CENEJPPESIJLEDHJAOJMNHZHZM—MMLJAR1C2CGEPC1T2T1T2TTPHJ1P2P1J2J3JJR

The Exodus – Session 7

Opening Prayer

Lord God we ask that you would bless this lesson so that we more fully understand your Word. Your Word is like a lamp that shines in the darkness of this world. It contains the answer to all of life's problems. Therefore, with your blessing we can draw closer to you and serve you more effectively. In Jesus's name we pray. Amen

Introduction

In the last session we reviewed many key events of Joseph's life, how he was sold into slavery and how he rose to the second most powerful leader in Egypt. For many centuries Egypt was the world's dominant political force. Joseph's brothers had intended to get rid of him because of their jealousy toward him. But God used those evil events for good because he placed Joseph in a position that, some years later, enabled him to help his family to prosper in Egypt. The book of Exodus begins where the book of Genesis leaves off. Exodus continues the record of the real and actual events of Abraham's descendents. Genesis 50 records the death of Joseph in about 1805 B.C. In this session we meet the new leader, Moses.

Session Material

1. (A) According to Exodus 12:40 how many years did Jacob's (Israel's) family and descendants live in Egypt? _____
(B) When Jacob's family first settled in Goshen in northern Egypt how many people were there in all according to Genesis 46:26-27 (Exodus 1:5)? _____

2. Based on the following verses from Exodus 1 described how the relationship changed between the new Pharaoh and Jacob's descendants.

Verses	Changes
6-7	
10	
11-12	
13	
14	
22	

3 According to the following verses from Exodus 2 note the key events of Moses' early life.

Verses	Key Events of Moses Life
1-2	
3	
5-10	
11-14	
15	
21-22	

4. Read Exodus 3:2-10. While in Midian what event occurred that would change Moses' life forever?

Verses	Event Details
1-3	
4-9	
10	

5. Based on the following passages how old was Moses at each of these events?

Passages	Moses' Events	Age
Acts 7:23-24	When he killed the Egyptian.	
Exodus 7:7	When he was called by God?	
Deuteronomy 34:7	When he died.	

6. According to Exodus 6:1-10 God wanted Moses to go to Pharaoh and demand what? _____

7. Read Exodus 7:3-5. Based on the following verses, why did Pharaoh refuse to let the people go? (Continued on the next page.)

Verses	Reasons
3	
5	

8. Ten times Moses and his brother Aaron went to Pharaoh to insist that he let the Israelites go. Each time Pharaoh refused. Based on the following passages from Exodus, what were the first nine plagues imposed on the Egyptians by God after each refusal?

Passages	Plagues
7:19	
8:5	
8:17	
8:24	
9:3-6	
9:9-11	
9:18	
10:12	
10:22	

Note: With the ninth plague, like all of the previous ones, none of them had an effect on the Israelites. Some of the plagues were a direct assault on the pagan Egyptian gods. For example the ninth plague "defeated" their sun god.

9. Even after all of these nine plagues what was Pharaoh's response to Moses according to Exodus 10:27-29? _____

_____

10. Based on Exodus 11:4-6 what was the tenth and final plague? _____

_____

11. Often the end of one thing marks the beginning of something new or different. The tenth plague marked the beginning of what would become a new and important religious event for the Israelites. It was to be celebrated annually forever as a reminder of God's mighty power as he rescued his people. Read about it in Exodus 12:1-14. This Passover event foreshadowed what other major event in history? See Matthew 26:17-28._____

_____

Note: The Feast of Unleavened Bread mentioned in Matthew 26:17 was another important religious event instituted by God to celebrate the Israelite's exodus from

Egypt. When we participate in the Lord's Supper (Communion), we need to be aware of the meaning of this event; that being that a spotless lamb had to shed its blood for the atonement of the people's sins. The Israelites were to eat the body of the sacrificed animal just as we eat the body and drink the blood of the one who was our sacrifice, Jesus Christ. He was without sin but he died on the cross for the forgiveness of the sins of all believers. He paid the price for the atonement of our sins.

12. The Passover event was enough for Pharaoh to finally let the Israelites go. After 430 years in Egypt they began their march to the Promised Land, the land that was promised to Abraham, Isaac, and Jacob in God's covenant with them. Based on Exodus 12:37-38 how many Israelites and other people left Egypt during the exodus event? _____

_____

13. According to Exodus 13:20-22 what/who escorted the Israelites on their journey out of Egypt?
(A) By day: _____
(B) By night: _____

Session 7 Discussion Questions

1. While in Midian Moses experienced a life-changing event. He experienced God in the burning bush. How can we experience life changing events too?

2. God hardened Pharaoh's heart and he bitterly refused any of God's instructions. Have you ever hardened your heart toward someone or something?

3. Joseph held no animosity toward his brothers for selling him into slavery. He expressed tears of joy, forgiveness, hope and love when they were reunited. How is this a good example for us to follow when we are wronged by someone?

Suggested Reading for Session 8

Exodus 14 through 31

Progress:

GELNDJJR1S2S1K2K1C2CENEJPPESIJLEDHJAOJMNHZHZM–MMLJAR1C2CGEPC1T2T1T2TTPHJ1P2P1J2J3JJR

Sojourn at Mount Sinai – Session 8

Opening Prayer

Lord God we do not deserve the many blessings you shower upon us. We are so blessed to be able to study your Word and yet, so many believers as well as nonbelievers ignore it. We ask that you continue to cause us to hunger and thirst for your Word because it is the source of all spiritual knowledge and truth. In Jesus's name we pray. Amen

Introduction

In the last session we saw how the Israelites went from being a friend of Egypt to being its slaves. God sent Moses to inflict ten plagues on Egypt to force Pharaoh to let the Israelites go. Finally the tenth plague, the Passover, was enough for Pharaoh to let the Israelites go. In this session we will review Israel's journey to Mount Sinai.

Session Material

1. As the Israelites were leaving Egypt following the Passover event, Pharaoh changed his mind and sent his army out to bring them back. Once again Pharaoh's heart was hardened. Read Exodus 14:9-31 to see how God protected his people from the Egyptian army. Based on verses 21- 22 what miraculous action did God use?_____

_____

Note: Note in Exodus 14:31 that it mentions the great work that was done by God to the Egyptian soldiers that did two things. First, it defeated the Israelite's enemy; and second, it demonstrated God's power. Some try to explain this event as a coincidence or luck that an east wind come along at the right time is to diminish what God did. Just remember that God controls all events in our lives too and we need to thank and praise him for his great mercy and his blessings.

2. About 45 days after leaving Egypt the Israelites started to grumble because of the lack of food and water. They were traveling in the north end of the inhospitable Sinai Desert. How did God provide for their needs based on the following passages from Exodus?

Passages	What did God Provide?
16:13	
16:14-15 & 31	
17:6	

3. The journey to the Promised Land was filled with many events. With Pharaoh and his army gone another foe appeared. According to the following verses from Exodus 17 answer the following questions.

Verses	Questions	Answers
8	Who was the foe?	
10	Who led Israel's troops?	
13	What was the outcome?	

Note: As you read in Exodus 17 you can see how God was involved in this battle. God was involved in every battle and problem his people experienced. In this reading we see another leader emerging from among the Israelites, Joshua.

Note: Many practical things needed to be established among this large group of Israelite people, some two million in all. A few months earlier they were in bondage to Egypt, the most powerful nation on earth. Now they were the people of an emerging nation of their own. How were they to administer law and order? They needed to develop a whole new culture. We saw how they were able to organize an army and defeat an enemy. No problem, God was with them.

4. Among his other duties Moses had taken on the duties of a judge to settle disputes. Read Exodus 18:15-24. What was Jethro's (Moses' father-in-law) idea?

_____

_____

Note: Within three months after leaving Egypt the Israelites arrived at Mount Sinai which was about 250 miles southeast of Goshen. (Mount Sinai lies about 50 miles north of the southern tip of the Sinai Peninsula.) They had to journey around mountains and other rough terrain; thus staying on a path suitable for travel for both young and old alike. The events that occurred at Mount Sinai are recorded in the rest of Exodus, all of Leviticus, and into the tenth chapter of Numbers. Note the location of Mount Sinai on a map; near the southern tip of the Sinai Peninsula.

5. In Exodus 19:3-7 God restated the covenant he first established with Abraham and his descendants about 600 years earlier. What is the one condition and the three major promises found in the covenant according to these verses from Exodus 19?

Verses	Condition and Promises
5a	Condition:
5b	
6a	
6b	

Note: The Israelites were God's chosen people. By accepting this covenant they were to become God's kingdom on earth and willingly do his work so that, through them, all of the nations on earth would be blessed. God blessed them to be a blessing to other people. God's people were to be set apart from the rest of the world. They were to be in the world but not part of what the world does. They were to lead holy lives and conduct themselves according to God's laws and statutes.

6. When Moses went down off the mountain and back to the Israelites, he told them of God's promises and conditions. What response did he get from them based on Exodus 19:8? _____

_____

7. According to Exodus 20:1-17, what did God give to Moses while he was on the mountain? _____

8. Based on Exodus 24:12 how did Moses receive the 10 Commandments form God? _____

9. We hear a lot about the 10 Commandments, but God also gave Moses many other laws and statutes for the purpose of establishing law and order and a system of justice. These laws and statutes form the foundation upon which our legal system is based today. According to the following passages from Exodus note what these laws and statutes pertained to.

Passages	Laws and Statutes
21:2-11	
21:12-36	
22:1-15	
22:16-31	
23:1-9	
23:10-13	
23:14-19	

10. Based on the following verses from Exodus 25 what did God want Moses to have the Israelites build?

Verses	Build What?	Meaning
8		A holy place set apart for worship.
9		A place where God dwells among his people.

11. In Exodus 25:10-22 God gave Moses detailed instructions for the construction of the Ark of the Covenant. Based on the following passages what was put into or near the Arc? (Continued on the next page.)

Passages	What was put in or near the Ark?
Exodus 16:33-34	
Exodus 25:16	
Numbers 17:10	

Note: Aaron's staff was symbolic of the house of Levi, one of the 12 tribes, who were set apart for the priesthood within the Israelite nation. Also, the staff was used as God's conduit for Moses and Aaron to do miracles. (See Exodus 4:17 and 7:8.)

Note: Exodus 25 through 31 describes many details of the construction of the Tabernacle and its furnishings; including the Ark of the Covenant. Everything had a practical use as well as a symbolic meaning.

Session 8 Discussion Questions

1. God was involved in every battle and problem his people experienced. Is God involved in our battles and problems today? If so why does he allow bad things to happen to believers?

2. Everything in the tabernacle had a practical use as well as a symbolic meaning. What are some of the furnishings in our churches?

3. God's people were to be set apart from the rest of the world. They were to be in the world but not part of what the world does. They were to lead holy lives and conduct themselves according to God's will. Does this still apply to Christians today?

Suggested Reading for Session 9

Exodus 32 through Leviticus 27

Progress:

GELNDJJR1S2S1K2K1C2CENEJPPESIJLEDHJAOJMNHZHZM–MMLJAR1C2CGEPC1T2T1T2TTPHJ1P2P1J2J3JJR

God Speaks to the Israelites – Session 9

Opening Prayer

Lord God we need you every hour of every day. You are an awesome God who protects us from the evil one and also blesses us with those things that we need. Keep us steadfast in your Word. Empower us to complete this complete study of your Word. May all we think, say, and do be acceptable to you. In Jesus's name we pray. Amen

Introduction

In the last session we saw how God saved the Israelites from Pharaoh's army during the crossing of the Red Sea. Then, after about three months they made their way to Mount Sinai where God gave the Ten Commandments to Moses and Moses taught them to the Israelites. In this session we will review some of the major laws, statutes, and regulations God gave to his people while at Mount Sinai.

Session Material

1. Moses spent two 40-day periods at the top of Mount Sinai with God. During the first trip to the mountain top notice what the Israelites did and what the consequences were based on the following verses from Exodus 32?

Verses	Questions	Answers
1-3	Who was the leader?	
4	What did he make?	
5-6	What did the Israelites do?	
19	How did Moses react?	
20	What happened to the calf?	
26-28	What did the Levites do?	
35	What did God do?	

2. Some time later Moses was summoned back to the top of Mount Sinai. Based on the following verses from Exodus 34 answer these questions about what happened during this 40-day period. (Continued on the next page.)

Verses	Questions	Answers
1a	What was Moses to do?	
1b	What was God going to do?	
6	What is the gist of God's proclamation?	
7	Why is God the just God?	
Note the three items added to the covenant:		
12	What was the first item added to the covenant?	
13	What was the second item added to the covenant?	
14	What was the third item added to the covenant?	

3. According to Exodus 35:1-3 what was God's command? _____

_____

Note: Exodus 35-40 deals mostly with the construction of the tabernacle and its furnishings. The tabernacle was where the Israelites were to worship God. It was to be portable because the Israelites were wanders in the wilderness for forty years. The requirement was to build everything exactly how God wanted it done. The value of the gold and silver used in the tabernacle has been valued at tens of millions of dollars, especially with today's valuation of precious metals.

4. Based on Exodus 40:34-38 what did God do to provide the Israelites guidance in their travels?_____

_____

_____

5. In the book of _____ we saw how mankind ruined his perfect relationship with God. In the book of _____ we saw how God established the Law and a plan for mankind's redemption. Next, in the book of Leviticus we will study how the Israelites were to live and worship God. Many of the laws, regulations, rules, and statutes were established during the year-long period the Israelites spent at Mount Sinai.

6. The book of Leviticus has a special theme which focuses on the appointment of the priests and the documentation of the many laws, statutes, and rituals that the Israelite priests were to act upon. Leviticus means that this book is related to the

_____ people. They were one of the twelve tribes of Israel (Jacob). This tribe was commissioned by God to fulfill the responsibilities of the priesthood. They were God's ambassadors to exercise the laws, regulations, rules, and statutes within and among God's chosen people.

7. Sin separates man from God. God put into place a way for the Israelites to atone for their sins. How can an unholy people maintain a close fellowship with a holy God? To provide a way, God developed five main types of offerings (sacrifices) to enable sinners a way to get right with God. There were others too. Based on the following passages from Leviticus, what are the names of the offerings established by God?

Passages	Offering Names	Main Purpose
1:13		Atonement for unintentional sin; and devotion to God
2:14-16		Recognize God's goodness and provision.
4:13-14		Forgiveness of certain sin.
5:14-16		Forgiveness of sins requiring restitution and cleansing from defilement.
7:12-13		Act of thanks and fellowship

8. Based on Leviticus 8:22 what key event occurred and why?
(A) Key event: _____
(B) Why: _____

_____

9. God also established eight main religious festivals as reminders to all of Israelite's believers of his love and mercy. Based on the following passages from Leviticus, name the eight main festivals instituted by God for the Israelites.
(Continued on the next page.)

Passages	Feast Name	Main Purpose
23:3 & 25:1-4		Rest for people, animals and land.
23:5-6		Remember God's deliverance.
23:9-10		Recognize God as the provider.
23:15-16		Thanksgiving for the harvest.
23:23-25		Day of rest to recognize God.
23:26-27		Cleanse people and priests, purify the Holy of Holies.

23:33		Remember the journey from Egypt and give thanks for the Promised Land.
25:10-13		Every 50th year help the poor.

Session 9 Discussion Questions

1. Exodus 35:1-3 records God's command to remember the Sabbath day and keep it holy. Many Christians attend church a couple of times a month or a few times per year. Is that level of performance in keeping with God's command?

Benefits of regular worship:

2. God punishes the guilty, even to the third and fourth generations (Exodus 34:7). Is that still the way it is today?

3. Moses burned the idol, ground it to dust, and made the people drink it down with water. How are our sins eliminated?

Suggested Reading for Session 10

Numbers 1 through 36

Progress:

GELNDJJR1S2S1K2K1C2CENEJPPESIJLEDHJAOJMNHZHZM–MMLJAR1C2CGEPC1T2T1T2TTPHJ1P2P1J2J3JJR

The Journey Continues – Session 10

Opening Prayer

Lord God you guided the Israelite's travels thorough the wilderness for 40 years. In the same way help and guide us though our life's journey. With knowledge of your Word and direction from the Holy Spirit, help us to make the correct decisions that will lead us into doing your will. Guide us to life's final destination, eternity with you. In Jesus's name we pray. Amen

Introduction

In the last session we discussed the main laws, statutes, and regulations God gave to the Israelites while still at Mount Sinai. We also reviewed the five major types of offerings and the eight major festivals God established that served as the foundation for worship and living as a people of God. Now with a method of worship and a plan of redemption solidly in place the Israelites were ready for the rest of their 40-year journey to the Promised Land. In this session we see the Israelites traveling forward to the Promised Land guided by God each step of the way.

Session Material

1. The year long stay at Mount Sinai saw God's chosen people growing in their faith; learning many new laws and regulations; and getting organized as an emerging nation. Based on the following passages in what ways were they getting organized?

Passages	Getting organized in what ways?
Exodus 18:24-26	
Numbers 1:2-3	
Numbers 1:51	
Numbers 1:52-53	
Numbers 2: 9, 16, 24, and 31	
Numbers 4:4, 24, and 31	
Numbers 8:23-26	
Numbers 11:16-17	

2. After almost 14 months from the time they left Egypt, the Israelites broke camp at Mount Sinai and set out for the Promised Land. Based on Numbers 10:33-34 how many days did they travel in this part of their journey? _____

3. Travel was very difficult for the Israelites given the hot climate, the hilly desert terrain, and the lack of "normal" food and water. Remember that there were about two million people. They did not need a grocery store; they needed a whole chain of grocery stores. But, God would provide for their needs. Based on these verses from Numbers 11, answer the following questions.

Verses	Questions	Answers
1	What was God's reaction to the complaints?	
10	What did the people continue to do?	
11-15	What did Moses do?	
31-34	What did God do?	1. 2.

4. Based on Numbers 12:16 what was the next stop-over for the Israelites?

_____

5. Over time the Israelites approached the southern edge of the Promised Land. Note the events that occurred based on the following passages from Numbers.

Passages	Events
13:1-2	
13:27-29	
13:30	
13:31-32	
14:5-9	
14:10	

6. The attitude and actions of the Israelites greatly impacted their future. Based on the following verses from Numbers 14 how did God respond to the lack of faith shown by most of the Israelites?

Verses	God's Responses
20	
21-24	
25	
29-32	
33-35	
36-38	

7. Based on Numbers 20:6-12 what did Moses do and what was God's reaction?
Moses: _____

God's reaction: _____

_____

8. The land was fully occupied in and around the Promised Land. Kings in those areas were fearful of the Israelites and were not eager to have them around. As they approached the Promised Land what were the results of each of the following military encounters, based on these passages from Numbers?

Passages	Kingdom of:	Results
20:20-21	Edom	
21:1-3	Arad	
Note: After the Israelites defeated Arad they continued their journey to the Promised Land but they took an indirect route around Edom (Numbers 21:4) which was about 200 miles out of their way.		
21:21-25 & 31-32	Amorites	
21:33-35	Bashan	

Note: After these encounters the Israelites traveled to the plains of Moab and camped along the east bank of the Jordan River, across from Jericho. From this location they would begin the conquest of the land on Canaan, their Promised Land. Locate the Jordan River and the city of Jericho on a map.

9. Because of Moses' sin he was not allowed to enter the Promised Land. Based on Numbers 27:12-22 who followed Moses as Israelite's new leader? _____

Note: After 40 years of hope, hardship, and healing the Israelites are now ready to enter the Promised Land.

Session 10 Discussion Questions

1. According to question number one above the Israelites spent a year learning God's laws and regulations. How long does it take a Christian to learn God's laws and commands?

2. In what ways do children suffer today because of the sins of their parents like the example found in Numbers 14:33?

3. Does it sometimes take a whole generation for a people to change like the 40 years of wandering and death in the desert?

Suggested Reading for Session 11

Deuteronomy 1-34 and Joshua 1-4

Progress:

GELNDJJR1S2S1K2K1C2CENEJPPESIJLEDHJAOJMNHZHZM–MMLJAR1C2CGEPC1T2T1T2TTPHJ1P2P1J2J3JJR

Entering the Promised Land – Session 11

Opening Prayer

Lord God, when we wonder about all of the things that you have created: the stars, the thunder, the mountains, the oceans, the land, the plants, the animals, and all of the people of the world, we realize how your mighty power through-out the universe is displayed. How great you are Lord! How great you are! To reveal your greatness we ask that you bless us as we study your Word. In Jesus's name we pray. Amen

Introduction

In the last session we reviewed events from about 38 of the 40 years the Israelites wandered in the wilderness. We saw how the sins of the Israelite people caused God to curse them with 38 more years of wandering in the wilderness. Even Moses' sin caused him to be excluded from entering the Promised Land. In the last session we left off with the Israelites encamped on the east side of the Jordan River, about five miles from Jericho. In this session we will see how the Israelites entered the Promised Land.

Session Material

1. The book of Deuteronomy begins where the book of Numbers leaves off. Deuteronomy is the fifth of the five books of Moses often referred to as the Pentateuch. Deuteronomy means "_____ _____". Moses repeats the whole law, thus reinforcing it as the foundation for all matters of faith and life for the Israelite people.

2. Based on Deuteronomy 3:23-26 what did Moses ask from God and how did God respond?
Moses' request: _____
God's response: _____

3. Based on the following verses from Deuteronomy 6 list the instructions Moses reemphasized with the people. (Continued on the next page.)

Verses	Instructions
5	
6	
7	
8-9	
13	
14	

18	

4. Read Deuteronomy 7:1-6. This passage provides a strong message about how the Israelites were to treat their enemies in Canaan, the Promised Land. Based on the following verses what were the Israelites to do?

Verses	Instructions
2	
3-4	
5	

5. Why did the Israelites treat the Canaanites so severely according to Deuteronomy 7:4-6 (also 13:6-11)? _____

_____

_____

6. The covenant God first made with Abraham then renewed with Isaac, Jacob, and Moses cemented God's relationship with his people. Why did God favor the Israelite people based on the following verses from Deuteronomy 7?

Verses	Reasons
6	
8-9	

Note: God delivers on his promises with his chosen people then and still today. Our promised land is heaven. The way we eventually get there is through faith in his son, Jesus.

7. Based on Deuteronomy 20:1-4 why were the Israelites to not be fearful as they were going into the Promised Land? _____

_____

Note: Throughout the book of Deuteronomy we can read how Moses, along with God's guidance, prepared the people for the great drama that was about to unfold; that being the entrance into the long awaited Promised Land. Deuteronomy 34 records Moses' death when he was 120 years old. Joshua then took over leadership of the Israelite people. His resume was impressive. He:

- Witnessed the plagues and deliverance from Egypt.
- Trained at Moses' side for 40 years.
- Witnessed many of God's miracles performed in the desert wilderness.

- Accompanied Moses to the top of Mount Sinai when God gave the Ten Commandments.
- Had some military leadership experience.
- Was faithful to God.

Note: The 40 years of wandering in the wilderness made a big impact on the Israelite people. For example they learned to:

- Live in the wilderness.
- Trust in God
- Properly worship and love God.
- Shed the pagan Egyptian cultural influences.

The old generation was gone and a young, expectant generation of Israelites stood ready for the blessing of a new homeland which was promised by God.

Note: In Deuteronomy 2-3 we reviewed the first few military campaigns of the Israelites. These victories provided them with a good staging area on the east side of the Jordan River, not far from Jericho, that would enable them to enter the Promised Land and begin its conquest.

8. Read Joshua 1:1-5 and record God's orders to Joshua. _____

_____

Note: Joshua 1:4 describes the size of the Promised Land. It would extend:

- From the desert (Negev) to Lebanon
- From the Great Sea (Mediterranean Sea) to the Euphrates River
- Through the Hittite country to the north (Turkey).

The overall size could have been about 500 miles by 200 miles wide.

9. Read Joshua 1:6-8 and fill in the key words from God's instructions to Joshua.

(A) Be _____ and _____.

(B) Obey all of the _____.

(C) Do not _____ from the _____.

(D) Meditate on the _____ day and night.

(E) If Joshua followed these instructions what did God promise to do? _____

_____

10. As recorded in Joshua 1:10-11 Joshua gives the order to prepare for war in three days. Based on Joshua 1:16-18 what was the response of the people?

_____

_____

11. Joshua sent two spies out ahead of them. Based on the following verses from Joshua 2, record the events that took place.

Verses	Events
1	
2-3	
4-5	
6	
8-13	
14	
23-24	

12. Because of Rahab's cooperation and new-found faith (Joshua 2:11) how did God bless her based on the following passages?

Passages	Blessings
Matthew 1:5	
Hebrews 11:31	
James 2:25-26	

Note: Rahab put herself in harm's way by protecting the spies from the king. She remained faithful. We too need to realize that God's forgiveness is real to all who come to faith in Jesus; no matter what they have done. We also need to know that there is only one unforgivable sin; that is the rejection of God.

13. Just as the Canaanites had heard about the miracle of the crossing of the Red Sea on dry ground, God again performs a miracle at the Jordan River. What was it based on Joshua 4:19-24?_____

_____

Session 11 Discussion Questions

1. Moses had pleaded with God to allow him to go into the Promised Land. But God refused. Is it possible for us to anger God this way too and miss out on a huge blessing because of our sins?

2. Read Deuteronomy 6:6-9. So parents, how well do you comply with this command?

3. God delivers on his promises with his chosen people then and still today. Our promised land is heaven. The way we eventually get there is through faith in his son, Jesus. We are still sinning today, but God has a new covenant with his people through Jesus. God is faithful and just, he forgives the sins of believers, and he grants to us eternal life. In what ways can we receive God's forgiveness?

4. What lesson does Joshua 1:7 provide to us as we live our daily lives?

Suggested Reading for Session 12

Joshua 5 through Judges 1

Progress:

GELNDJJR1S2S1K2K1C2CENEJPPESIJLEDHJAOJMNHZHZM-MMLJAR1C2CGEPC1T2T1T2TTPHJ1P2P1J2J3JJR

Conquering the Promised Land – Session 12

Opening Prayer

Lord God, your name alone is worthy to be praised. You build us up and help us when the troubles of this life inflict us. You heal us and bind our wounds. Lord, you determined the number of stars and call each one by name. Great is your love toward us. Help us to continue digging deeper into your Word. Help us complete this study so we more fully know you. All of this we do for your glory and in Jesus's name we pray. Amen

Introduction

In the last session we reviewed the fifth book of Moses, the book of Deuteronomy. In that book Moses repeated the whole law to the Israelites. Further, they were instructed to go into Canaan; take the land by force; and take no prisoners. After Moses' death, Joshua became the leader of the Israelites. In this session we will see how the Israelites begin the conquest of the Promised Land.

Session Material

1. After the Israelites crossed the Jordan River on dry ground they camped about two miles from Jericho. Upon God's command and using God's military tactics the Israelite army attacked Jericho. Based on the following verses from Joshua 6, answer the following questions.

Verses	Questions	Answers
17	Who was to be spared?	
21	Who was not to be spared?	
24a	What happened to Jericho?	
24b	What happened to precious artifacts?	

2. The Israelites next battle would be at Ai, about five miles from Jericho. According to Joshua 8:24-29 what was the outcome? _____

_____

Note: After the fall of Jericho and Ai other kings in the northern part of the region felt threatened because of the Israelite's military successes. According to Joshua 9:1-2, other northern kings formed an alliance in an attempt to overpower and defeat the Israelites. The conditions in the region at that time were very tense. At this time the whole area is only about 200 miles long and 90 miles wide.

3. The Gibeonites lived about 10 miles from Jericho. They were a clever people. They saw what was happening to the kingdoms around them so they tricked the Israelites into making a treaty with them even though God had previously told them to make no treaties with anyone from the land of Canaan. According to Joshua 9:26-27 in return for not killing them what did the Gibeonites agree to do?

_____

4. In the southern region of the Promised Land five kings from the Amorite peoples agreed to band together against the Israelites. Read Joshua 10:9-15. What was the outcome of the battle based on the following verses from Joshua 10?

Verses	Outcomes
10	
11	
13-14	

5. Joshua went on to "mop-up" the southern cities in the area. Read Joshua 10:40-42. Why were Joshua and his army so successful?_____

_____

6. Joshua 11 recorded another major battle, this time against the kings who formed the northern alliance. Based on the following verses from Joshua 11, answer these questions.

Verses	Questions	Answers
4	How large was their army?	
7-8	What was the outcome?	
14	What was done with the plunder and livestock?	
18	Over how many years did the battles occur?	

7. Based on Joshua 12:24 how many kingdoms were conquered by the Israelites up to this point? _____

8. Based on Joshua 11:20 God showed no mercy on the Canaanite people. Why?

_____

Note: The first commandment tells us that we shall believe in the only God, the creator of everything. We are to worship no other gods. God is a jealous God and wants no competition. Matthew 4:10 says that we are to worship the Lord, and him only should we serve. In Isaiah 42:8 we are told: "I am the Lord; that is my name; and my glory will I not give to another, neither my praise to graven images."

Note: The way God used his chosen people to eliminate the sinful Canaanite people can be troubling as we study these brutal accounts of war. But, God will allow sin to enter in his creation for a season. If gone unrepented God's wrath builds and his justice gets dispensed. God's actions are just. He used Joshua and his army to take the land of Canaan away from a sinful people who worshiped false gods in order to establish a holy nation devoted to him. The Israelites were to become the beacon for the rest of the world. The Israelites were blessed to be a blessing to other peoples of the world. God did not order Joshua to conquer the whole world. Only a small part of it needed to be cleansed of all paganism in order to serve God's purposes.

9. God dispensed his justice on the Canaanites. There will be a time when God's patience wears out and justice will be served once and for all. What event will occur that will bring an end to evil according to Revelation19:11-21?

_____

Note: For a time God is using his people to reach out to the rest of the unbelieving world. One day evil will wage one last battle with God and his people. We already know what the outcome will be. Satan and his followers will be defeated forever. All who believe will receive their promised reward, spending eternity with God.

10. (A) According to Joshua 13:1-6 was all of the Promised Land conquered and cleansed yet? _____
(B) Why was it important to conquer the rest of the land? _____

_____

Note: Joshua 13:7 through 22:34 describes how the Promised Land was distributed among the twelve tribes of Israel. Each tribe was given land except the tribe of Levi.

11. Joshua's last key pronouncement is recorded in Joshua 24:14-15. What was his challenge that everyone must act upon? _____

_____

12. After Joshua's death the leaders from the tribe of Judah continued to "mop-up" remaining pagan kingdoms and tribes. Eventually armies from the other Israelite tribes also engaged the pagan enemy. According to the following verses from Judges 1 were they always successful in eliminating the enemy? (Continued on the next page.)

Verses	Successful?	Tribe
4		Judah

51

8		Judah (Jerusalem)
10		Judah
11-13		Othniel (Judge)
17		Judah
18		Judah
19		Judah
21		Benjamin
22 & 25		Joseph
27		Manasseh
28		Israelites
29		Ephraim
30		Zebulun
31-32		Asher
33		Naphtali
34		Dan
35		Joseph

Note: Even though they defeated much of the Canaanite lands, remnants of resistance still remained. But, God wanted the whole Promised Land to be cleansed of all residue of paganism; not just some of it. Israel did not comply.

Session 12 Discussion Questions

1. In Joshua 24:14-15 is recorded the profound decision every living person must make: Choose for yourself right now who you will serve, God or man.
   - I choose to serve _____ !

2. The first commandment warns us not to have other gods. What are some of the other gods that people serve today?

3. War is a terrible curse that we bring on ourselves. What are some of the motives for war?

4. The fifth commandment says that we are not to kill others. How is it then that God uses war as a means to an end?

Reading Assignment for Session 13

Judges 2 through Ruth 4

Progress:

GELNDJJR1S2S1K2K1C2CENEJPPESIJLEDHJAOJMNHZHZM-MMLJAR1C2CGEPC1T2T1T2TTPHJ1P2P1J2J3JJR

The Judges of Israel – Session 13

Opening Prayer

Lord God, you were Israel's helper in ages past and you are our hope for years to come. Will you be our guard when troubles come? Many times have you delivered your people, long ago and even yet today. As we study your Word, keep us steadfast and focused so we can more deeply appreciate and comprehend your loving grace. In Jesus's name we pray. Amen

Introduction

In the last session we studied about how the Israelites entered the Promised Land and fought over 30 military campaigns against the many pagan kingdoms that resided there. The Israelites were to defeat the Canaanites, make no treaties with them, and remain faithful to God. We saw how they failed on all three counts. In this session we see the repercussions of their failure to keep their covenant with God.

Session Material

1. Up to this point in Israel's existence as a nation, they had no formal government structure. They were a tight knit group of 12 interdependent tribes who all shared a faith in the one true God. That was the glue that held them together as a people with a common purpose and destiny. The type of government they did have is referred to as a _____. It means that God himself was in control. God chose the leaders and directed their actions.

Note: A brief definition of a theocracy is when a government's leaders are divinely guided. All of Israel's leaders up to this point in their history had been divinely guided. Abraham, Isaac, Jacob, Moses, and Joshua were examples.

Note: In the last session we noted that most of the 12 tribes were involved in military skirmishes with Canaanites who had survived the previous wars. The Israelites failed to totally conquer the Promised Land as God had commanded them to do.

2. In the first chapter of the book of Judges, 17 skirmishes between the Israelites and the Canaanites are mentioned. Ten of the skirmishes were not victorious for Israel. Read Judges 2:8-15. Why was God withholding his complete power from the Israelites based on the following verses from Judges 2? (Continued on the next page.)

Verses	Outcomes
10	

11-12a	
12b-13	
And the consequences were:	
14-15	- - -

Note: The Israelites picked up bad habits from the remnant of the Canaanites that lived with and around them. They worshiped false gods, Baal being one of them. Baal worship involved the worship of idols, "sacred" prostitution, and even child sacrifice. Ashtoreths were female goddesses like were Venus and Aphrodite who encouraged immoral behavior in the guise of a religion.

3. The Israelite's relationship with God was strained; but when hearing the Israelite's pleas for help from oppression, God would raise up judges who would deliver them from their enemies. The book of Judges records many cycles of Israelite unfaithfulness and faithfulness (oppression followed by peace). Over a period of about 300 years after Joshua's death a number of judges were raised up to restore Israel from oppression because of their unfaithfulness. Who were six of the prominent judges based on the following passages from the book of Judges?

Passages	Years of Oppression	Judge's Names	Years of Peace
3:9-11	8		40
3:12-30	18		80
4:1-24; 5:31	20		40
6:7-8:28	7		40
10:8; 11:1-33; 12:7	18		6
13:1,15:1-20	40		20

4. Judges 13-16 reads like a novel about Samson's life, from birth through his death. He was one of the judges and had many unique life experiences. According to the following passages from Judges what were some of the key events of his life? (Continued on the next page.)

Passages	Samson's Events
15:14-15	
16:16-17	
16:21	

16:29-30	

5. According to Judges 17:6 what two pieces of information are mentioned that help explain the conditions in Israel during this period of time (about 1055 B.C.)?

(A) _____.

(B) _____.

Note: The people had been demanding to have a king. This demand undermined God's plan for his chosen people. Many Israelites had departed from God's standards and rules of conduct. They became easily led astray by the influence of the pagan people still within and around the Promised Land.

6. Judges 19-20 describe the deplorable conditions that existed in Israel at the time. Many were doing "as they saw fit". For example, describe what happened based on the following verses from Judges 19?

Verses	Events
1	
22	
23-25	
26-28	
29-30	

Note: The most likely reason for the Levites to do this grotesque act was to create awareness and get the attention of the Israelites. The concubine had died as a result of the brutal treatment she had received. They needed a wakeup call to realize the moral degeneracy into which they had slipped. The behavior of the Levite man was also detestable. Was he punished for his complicit behavior? Did he do everything he could to protect his concubine?

7. How did the Israelites respond to these horrible acts committed against the concubine according to the following verses from Judges 20? (Continued on the next page.)

Verses	Events
9-11	

12-13	
After three days of battle against the Benjamites, who won?	
35	
48	

8. Concern for the tribe of Benjamin's near annihilation is recorded in Judges 21. According to verses 20-25 what was the two part plan to restore the Benjamites?

(A) _____ .

(B) _____ .

Note: The repopulation of the towns within the tribe of Benjamin involved the abduction of women. The book of Judges records these dastardly deeds done by the Israelites to show the depths of sin to which Israel had sunk. This serves as an example for us to see what happens to people who forget and reject God. When people are focused on the world, loss and chaos will result. What is wrong by God's standards will be acceptable to a sinful world. But, God, who is faithful and just, will forgive us of our sins if we repent and turn back to him.

9. Not everything during the 300 year period of Israel's judges was a disaster. The book of Ruth records many of Ruth's acts of selfless love toward her mother-in-law. Ruth was from Moab, not an Israelite. Her pronouncement in Ruth 1:16-17 exposed her true character.
(A) What did she announce? _____
(B) How was she blessed according to Matthew 1:5 and 16? _____

Session 13 Discussion Questions

1. A theocracy is a form of government when its leaders are divinely guided by a supreme religious leader. In Israel's case, God was the supreme leader. What can happen to a nation who refuses to obey God's laws and statutes?

2. Why did God withhold his complete power from the Israelites and from us today?

3. Many Israelites had departed from God's standards and rules of conduct. They became easily led astray by the influence of the pagan people still within and around the Promised Land. Can the same thing happen today?

4. These events from the book of Judges provide a lesson for all of mankind. Without a moral foundation to base our laws and actions, "everyone will do as they see fit". How do people do whatever they see fit today?

Suggested Reading for Session 14

1 Samuel 1 through 2 Samuel 5

Progress:

GELNDJJR1S2S1K2K1C2CENEJPPESIJLEDHJAOJMNHZHZM-MMLJAR1C2CGEPC1T2T1T2TTPHJ1P2P1J2J3JJR

From Judges to Kings – Session 14

Opening Prayer

Lord God, we ask your blessing on us as we continue to study your Word. We ask that you guide us and sustain us so that as we study, we worship your greatness in truth and purity. We lift up our souls to you because we trust you. We give you thanks for many blessings already received because of your grace. In Jesus's name we pray. Amen

Introduction

In the last session we reviewed several of the judges God raised up to lead the Israelites in the military skirmishes that occurred. Remnants of various Canaanite kingdoms remained in the Promised Land. God allowed Israel to lose some of the military skirmishes because of their apostasy. The Israelites intermarried with the pagan people. Many Israelites worshiped false gods. In this session we see how the Israelites cry out for a king and forsake their real King.

Session Material

1. In the southwestern part of the Promised Land was the region known as Philistia. It was about 60 miles long and about 15 miles wide. It was located along the eastern shore of the Great (Mediterranean) Sea. According to Judges 1:18 name the three cities captured by the Israelites prior to the period of the judges, about 1200 B.C.
(1) _____ (2)_____ (3) _____
The other two main cities in Philistia were Ashdod and Gath.

2. According to Judges 15:14-16 and 20 which judge battled the Philistines?

_____

3. The region known as Philistia has been coveted by many over most of history and is still a hotly contested piece of real estate today. Its shipping ports and other commercial traffic routes made it an important link between areas we call today: Europe, Asia, and Africa. Over 300 years later the Philistine menace continued to plague the Israelites. According to 1 Samuel 4:10-11 what two key events occurred?
(1) _____.

(2) _____.

4. God raised up another leader for the Israelites. According to the following passages from 1 Samuel who was the man and to what three positions of leadership was he called? (Continued on the next page.)

Passages	Positions of Leadership
3:19	Who?
3:20	1 -
7:9	2 -
7:15-17	3 -

5. Read 1 Samuel 4:5-8. This passage reveals the respect the Philistines had for the God of the Israelites. How long did the Philistines have the Arc of the Covenant before returning it to the Israelites according to 1 Samuel 6:1? _____ This was a very serious matter for the Israelites because the Arc was a direct link to God's presence with them. Without it the Israelites felt lost and defeated.

6. According to 1 Samuel 7:10-13 what was the outcome of Samuel's encounters with the Philistines? _____

_____

7. Based on 1 Samuel 8:1-3 who followed Samuel as Israel's next judges and how well did they perform?
Who: _____

Performance: _____

8. The Israelites continued to demand that Samuel appoint a king. According to 1 Samuel 8:4-5 for what three reasons did they want a king?

Reason #	Reasons
1	
2	
3	

9. Based on 1 Samuel 8:6-9 what were the reactions of Samuel and God about Israel wanting an earthly king?
Samuel: _____

God: _____

_____

_____

Note: 1 Samuel 8:11-17 records the burdens that will be imposed in order to have a king. They include:
- Sons called into service to care for horses and chariots; some will be military commanders; some will be farmers; and some will required to make weapons.
- Daughters will be required to work as cooks and bakers.

- These things will be required for the king: the best vineyards and olive groves; one tenth of the grain crop; the best cattle and donkeys; and one tenth of the flocks.
- Many will become like slaves, in service to the king.

10. According to 1 Samuel 8:19 and 22 what was the peoples' response and God's response about having a king; even though they were warned about the burdens that they would face?

People: _____

God: _____

Note: God permitted the Israelites to have a king like the surrounding pagan nations. This marked still another occasion where the Israelites rejected the advice of their true King. God wanted his chosen people to be unlike other nations; not like them. With an earthly king Israel would transform its form of government from a theocracy to a monarchy.

11. (A) According to 1 Samuel 10:1 who did Samuel anoint as Israel's first king in about 1050 B.C.? _____
(B) Based on the following passages from 1 Samuel what do we know about this person?

Passages	Personal Attributes
9:1-2	
9:15-16	
10:6	
13:1	

12. While Saul was successful in a number of military campaigns he began to fall out of God's favor. Based on the following passages from 1 Samuel what wrong and improper actions did Saul do? (Continued on the next page.)

Passages	Saul's Actions
13:8-14	
14:24	

15:7-11	

13. In 1 Samuel 15:10-11, 26, and 35 it is recorded that God grieved that he had made Saul king because of his sins and disobedience.
(A) According to 1 Samuel 16:13 who would eventually become Israel's second king? _____.
(B) According to 1 Samuel 16:14 how did God deal with Saul, Israel's first disobedient king? _____.
(C) According to 1 Samuel 16:21-22 describe David's initial relationship with Saul.

_____

14. According to 1 Samuel 17:4-50 what event raised David's prominence within the Israelite nation? _____

Note: David's popularity with the people aroused Saul's jealousy toward him. 1 Samuel 19-26 records least 10 times that Saul attempted to kill David. Read Psalms 37 and 59. They record David's thoughts about these events and his prayers for deliverance during this period of his life.

15. Saul's life was marked with great victories for the Israelites. But, his many low points tainted his tenure as Israel's first king. According to 1 Samuel 31:1-7 how did Saul's kingship finally end? _____

_____

16. Based on 2 Samuel 2:1-4 what happened to David after Saul's death? _____

_____

Note: Judah comprised much of the southern part on the Israelite nation. Judah was loyal to David whose family was from Bethlehem in Judah. The rest of the 12 tribes of Israel to the north (within Canaan) were still loyal to the ruminant of King Saul's army. At this time in history Israel was divided over this issue.

17. Based on 2 Samuel 3:1 how long did the war between the southern tribes (Judah and Simeon) and northern tribes (Israel) last? _____

Note: 2 Samuel 5 records the civil war between the north and south of Israel; similar to the Civil War fought in the United States in the 1860's. But the war ended because they realized they had many things in common:
- They were family, descendants of Abraham, Isaac, and David.
- Together they were God's chosen people.
- They saw how God was with David. He was a great leader.
- They came to realize that God made him king.

18. How long did David reign as king over all of Israel according to 2 Samuel 5:4?

_____

Session 14 Discussion Questions

1. Joel and Abijah, Samuel's sons were dishonest, took bribes, and perverted justice. What can Christian parents do to help our children from becoming disobedient and evil?

2. Notice in 1 Samuel 8:6-8 that God granted his peoples' request for a king. Up to this point God was their King. Can God change his own mind? Why?

3. 1 Samuel 8:11-17 records the burdens that were imposed on the Israelites in order to have a king. What needs to be our attitude to our government with high taxes and wasteful spending?

4. Saul's life was marked with great victories for the Israelites. But, his many low points tainted his tenure as Israel's first king. How is this a good lesson for Christians today?

Suggested Reading for Session 15

2 Samuel 6 through 1 Kings 4
Read at least a chapter a day from the book of Psalms until completed.

Progress:

GELNDJJR1S2S1K2K1C2CENEJPPESIJLEDHJAOJMNHZHZM-MMLJAR1C2CGEPC1T2T1T2TTPHJ1P2P1J2J3JJR

Kings David, and Solomon – Session 15

Opening Prayer

Lord God, may your name be praised in all of the earth. May Bible studies like this one help us grow in the knowledge of your plan for mankind, for greater wisdom, and for insights we need to effectively witness to the lost. May all of this be done to glorify your name. In Jesus's name we pray. Amen

Introduction

In the last session we studied the events that led up to Israel's first king. The Israelites wanted an earthly king even though the cost to them was going to be high. Upon God's command Samuel anointed Saul as their first king. David succeeded Saul as Israel's second king. In this session we will review many events of David's reign as king and who was to succeed him.

Session Material

1. Early into David's reign Israel split into the northern alliance loyal to King Saul's army and the southern alliance loyal to King David. David was able to reunite the 12 tribes back into a single nation. Based on 2 Samuel 5:6-10 what was the significance of the battle against the Jebusites? _____

_____._____

_____

Note: Jerusalem was on the border of the land of Benjamin of the northern alliance and the land of Judah of the southern alliance. This particular area was not really controlled by either the northern or the southern tribes; similar to Washington D.C., a neutral part of the region. Jerusalem was only about eleven acres in size at the time and had a population of about 3500 people. Even though small in size Jerusalem would become a very important city in all of history.

2. Based on 2 Samuel 6:12 what was one on David's top priorities once he had moved into Jerusalem?_____

_____

3. In 2 Samuel 7:16 what did God promise to David? _____

_____

4. The covenant made with Abraham and renewed many times to his descendants was that Israel would be blessed and would become a blessing to people all around the world. This would become a reality with the birth, life, and death of God's only Son, Jesus Christ. Jesus was born of the Israelite tribe of Judah. According to Isaiah 9:6-7 from who would Jesus become a direct descendant?

_____

5. Based on the following passages from 1 and 2 Samuel list the kingdoms that David conquered in addition to the Jebusites in Jerusalem. Note that the numbers correlate to each of the kingdoms.

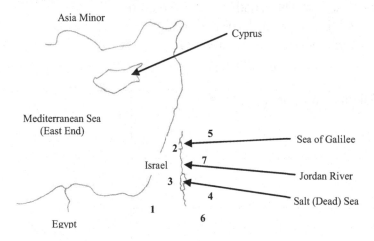

East End of the Mediterranean Sea and the Promised Land

#	Passages	Kingdoms
1	1 Samuel 30:17-18	
2	2 Samuel 5:11-25	
3	2 Samuel 8:1	
4	2 Samuel 8:2a	
5	2 Samuel 8:5	
6	2 Samuel 8:13-14	
7	2 Samuel 12:30-31	

6. The comment in 2 Samuel 8:6b sums up David's military career. What was it?

_____

Note: With the 12 tribes of Israel unified under King David, Jerusalem established as their capitol and worship center, and virtually all of the Promised Land conquered, Israel had become a prominent nation in the world. Their prosperity reached a new high because David followed God and God kept his promises to him.

7. Read Psalm 27 and describe David's relationship with God._____

_____

Note: David faced many dangers in his lifetime. Saul tried to kill him many times. He was in many military conflicts. He faced Goliath, the giant. In all of his troubles he turned to God. A nation is truly blessed to have its leaders turn to God for wisdom and leadership. Woe to those who don't.

8. Israel did not always prosper because of their sin. David had his successes and failures because he too was vulnerable to sin. Based on the following passages from 2 Samuel and one from 1 Kings, what were some of the failures and consequences?

Passages	David's Failures and Consequences
3:2-5	
11:1-5	
11:14-17	
11:27	
12:7-10	
12:15-18	
12:24	
13:28-29	
15:10-16	
18:14	
20:1-2 & 22	
1 Kings 2:13-25	

Note: According to 2 Samuel 19:43 Israel's ten northern tribes and the two southern tribes (Judah and Simeon) still did not fully get along. They were united but relations were strained. Greed and jealousy were the root causes of their disputes. If only they could have realized they had more in common than they had in differences.

9. David was a repentant sinner. He faced many tragic events. Understanding his life helps us to better understand the Psalms he wrote. His life, which was filled

with ups and downs, was reflected in his words in Psalm 23 which he wrote. Read Psalm 23 and note at least three ways in which this Psalm reflected his faith.

(1) _____.

(2) _____.

(3) _____.

10. David kept Israel away from idolatry and faithful to God. Even though David was sinful he always went back to the bed-rock of his faith through repentance. Based on Acts 13:22-23 how did God bless him?_____

_____

Note: Matthew 1:17 records Jesus' genealogy (through his earthly father, Joseph) in the following manner: Note the prominence of King David.
- From Abraham to King David – 14 generations
- From King David to the Babylonian exile – 14 generations
- From the Babylonian exile to Jesus – 14 generations

11. According to 1 Kings 1:29-30 who succeeded King David as Israel's next king?

_____

12. At about 20 years old Solomon began his kingship over the united Israelite nation in about 970 B.C. According to 1 Kings 3:1 what were five of his top priorities as the new king?

#	Top Priorities
1	
2	
3	
4	
5	

13. Read 1 Kings 3:5-15. How did God promise to bless Solomon according to the following verses?

Verses	God's Blessings on Solomon
12	
13	
14	

14. How did Solomon use the gifts and talents God gave him based on these verses from 1 King 4? (Continued on the next page.)

Verses	What Solomon Did
32	
33	
34	

Session 15 Discussion Questions

1. The Lord gave David victory everywhere he went. The Lord was with David in his many military conquests. The Lord is with us too when we are out fighting our daily battles. Why are we not always victorious?

2. The Israelites' prosperity reached a new high because David followed God and God kept his promises. If we had truly righteous leaders in our country today, would God bless us with prosperity?

3. A nation is truly blessed to have its leaders turn to God for wisdom and leadership. Woe to those who don't. In the United States the founding fathers realized the importance of God in the establishment of our nation. In what ways did they demonstrate their faith in God?

4. Israel's twelve tribes still did not fully get along with each other. Relations were strained. Greed and jealousy were the root causes of their disputes. If only they could have realized they had more in common than they had in differences. How does that apply to us today?

Suggested Reading for Session 16

1 Kings 5-17, Ecclesiastes 1-12, and Song of Songs 1-8
Read at least chapter a day from the book of Proverbs.

Progress:

GELNDJJR1S2S1K2K1C2CENEJPPESIJLEDHJAOJMNHZHZM-MMLJAR1C2CGEPC1T2T1T2TTPHJ1P2P1J2J3JJR

King Solomon and Other Kings – Session 16

Opening Prayer

Lord God you reign over all. The whole earth should rejoice and be glad! Righteousness and justice are the foundation of your throne. You will someday consume the foe on all sides and in every way. For you oh Lord, are the Most High over all the earth. You are exalted far above all gods. Those who love you Lord hate evil, for you guard the lives of the faithful and deliver us from the hand of the evil one. Guard and lead us as we continue this Bible study. In Jesus's name we pray. Amen (Psalm 97)

Introduction

In the last session we studied how God had blessed King David's reign by defeating all seven major kingdoms within the Promised Land. David was a sinful man but he remained faithful to God. He kept Israel away from idolatry. His son, Solomon, replaced him as king. Solomon was blessed with wisdom, riches, honor and long life. In this session we will review the rest of Israel's kings.

Session Material

1. Solomon spoke 3000 proverbs and wrote 1005 songs; studied plant and animal life; and was respected for his great wisdom by all other kings. He built the royal palace, the temple, and the wall around Jerusalem. He took Israel to a new peak in its prominence and prosperity. Three of his books are found in the Bible. See if you can name the books based on the clues provided for each of them.
(A) _____ - In this book Solomon wrote many rules for proper living. Many of the fundamental truths are short and to the point precepts about proper human behavior. Read 1:1-7 from this book. Note that it begins with the need for us to gain wisdom; realizing that the _____ of the _____ is the beginning of knowledge. From this book also read 22:1-29. This passage gives us examples of wise living and contrasts the _____ and the _____ person. Anyone who intends to be a true Christian and live a righteous life should make this your handbook for daily use. It needs to be read, studied and applied to daily living.

(B) _____ - In this book Solomon provides a philosophy for life. Vanity of vanities, all is vanity. When you die everything you have or did is gone or given away. Therefore, man cannot find true happiness apart from God. Solomon, with his 700 wives and 300 concubines; his great wealth; and his great wisdom claimed that we need to be happy with what we have and enjoy what God has given us. What are the key messages from each of the following passages from this book? (Continued on the next page.)

Passages	Messages
3:1-14	
5:10-12 and 18-20	
9:7-10 (Also Colossians 3:23)	

(C) _____ - Solomon's third book can be viewed as an allegory which uses symbolism to explain God's relationship with his faithful people and with his the church. Like the love between husband and wife, so to God loves his people and his church. What examples of God's love are recorded in these passages?

Passages	Examples of God's Love
John 3:16	
1 John 4:7-10	

2. Read 1 Kings 9:3-9. God speaks to Solomon in the 24th year of his reign, in about 946 B.C. Note the "if/then" points of God's message found in the following verses.

Verses	God's Main If /Then Points:	
4-5	If...	
	Then...	
6-7	If....	
	Then....	

3. According to the following verses from 1 Kings 10 how much wealth and splendor did Solomon accumulate? (Continued on the next page.)

Verses	Solomon's Wealth
14	
15	

22	
23	
25	
26	
27	

4. Israel was at its highest point in all of its history. But, evil has a way of reducing greatness into rubble. Many vices from the lifestyle Solomon lived eventually steered him away from God. The root causes of Solomon's apostasy are found in 1 Kings 11:1-6. What were they? _____ , _____ , and _____ .

5. The Lord was angry with Solomon because of his sins. Based on 1 Kings 11:11 and 31-33 what happened as a consequence?_____

_____

6. According to the following passages how long did the united Israelite nation last? Fill in the names of the kings and how long each one reigned.

Passages	Number of Years	Kings
Acts 13:21		
2 Samuel 5:4		
1 Kings 11:42		
Total Years		

Note: In the years that followed King Solomon's reign, Israel's prosperity would fall and then again rise; but never reaching the panicle they experienced during Solomon's reign. Now the Israelite nation was divided again. They gradually diminished in power and geographical influence. More importantly, Israel's faith in the one true God also diminished.

Note: The northern Israelite tribes lasted about 208 years and were destroyed by Assyria in 722 B.C. The southern tribes (Judah) lasted about 345 years and were destroyed by Babylon in about 586 B.C. During those years the northern tribes had 20 kings and the southern tribes also had 20 kings beyond Solomon's reign.

7. Each of the kings is discussed in both books of the Kings. Documentation is given about their faithfulness (or lack thereof) to God. As was the faith of the king so went the faithfulness of many of the people in the kingdom. For example, read 1 Kings 16:30 and note how King Ahab's faith is documented. _____

_____

Note: Just how deep was the sacrilege of all 40 kings after Solomon? Of the 20 northern kings 20 were unfaithful to God. Of the 20 southern kings

12 were unfaithful. This means that only eight of 40 kings (20%) were faithful to God.

8. Based on the following passages from 1 Kings who did King Ahab marry and what were some of their actions?

Passages	Actions
16:31	
16:32	
16:33	
18:4	

9. The reign of King Ahab along and his evil wife, Jezebel, marked a low point in Israel's spiritual relationship with God. As a result what did God have Elijah do based on 1 Kings 17:1? _____

Note: The drought was significant because the pagan god, Baal, was shown to be powerless against the one true God. Baal was considered to be the god of fertility, storm, and rain by the pagans. The ground was not very fertile without rain. Even this was not enough to turn people's hearts back toward God.

Session 16 Discussion Questions

1. Evil has a way of reducing greatness into rubble. Many vices from Solomon's lifestyle steered him away from God. If we are not careful we too can fall away from God. What are some of the reasons that can happen to us today?

2. Israel's prosperity gradually diminished in power and geographic influence. More importantly, Israel's faith in the one true God also diminished. Is there a correlation between faithfulness of a nation's leaders and its prominence and success?

3. The three year drought was significant because the pagan god, Baal, was shown to be powerless against the one true God. Baal was considered to be the god of fertility by the pagans. The ground was not very fertile without rain. Even

this was not enough to turn people's hearts back toward God. What does it take to turn hearts toward the Lord?

Suggested Reading for Session 17

1 Kings 18 through 2 Kings 25
Review the 17 prophetic books beginning with Isaiah and ending with Malachi to become familiar with these Old Testament prophets.

Progress:

GELNDJJR1S2S1K2K1C2CENEJPPESIJLEDHJAOJMNHZHZM-MMLJAR1C2CGEPC1T2T1T2TTPHJ1P2P1J2J3JJR

The End of a Blessing – Session 17

Opening Prayer

Lord God you are our King and our only God. You order our personal victories in life when you defeat those who would harm us. We need to be aware of the fact that, what we do, does not bring us victory; but you bring us victory over our enemies through your Son, Jesus. In your name we make our boast all day long. We praise your name forever. Guide us in our studies so we can more fully comprehend what you do for us each day. In Jesus's name we pray. Amen (Psalm 44)

Introduction

In the last session we studied about the spiritual condition of Israel. Solomon and many of the next 40 Israelite kings over the following generations worshiped pagan gods. We also reviewed the three other books written by Solomon. Finally we also reviewed some events of one of Israel's evil kings, Ahab, along with his evil wife, Jezebel. In this session we will complete our review of Israel's kings and look at events that immediately followed that time period in their history.

Session Material

1. God sent Elijah to prophesy in Israel over a period of about 15 years up to about 850 B.C. In the last session we discussed the apostasy of Israel. Elijah was one of many prophets God raised up to awaken Israel out of their spiritual sleep. Many of Elijah's experiences are recorded in 1 Kings 17 through 2 Kings 2. Based on the following verses from 1 Kings18 what events occurred at Mount Carmel?

Verses	Key Events
18-19	
23-24	
25-29	
30-35	
36-38	
39	
40	
45	

2. Based on the following passages answer the following questions pertaining to Elijah. (Continued on the next page.)

Passages	Questions	Answers
1 Kings 19:19-21	Who did Elijah call into God's services?	
2 Kings 2:11-12	How did Elijah's ministry end?	
Matthew 17:1-3	What event occurred?	

3. After Elijah's departure to heaven, Elisha's prophetic ministry began to flourish. His ministry lasted almost 50 years and was marked with several miracles that God used him to perform. Based on the following passages from 2 Kings what were some of those miracles?

Passages	Miracles
2:19-22	
4:1-7	
4:32-37	
4:38-41	
5:13-14	
6:3-7	

4. Based on 2 Kings 8:16-19 what was God's attitude toward the people of Judah even though their king was evil? _____

_____

Note: Most of the 40 kings after Solomon were not faithful to God. The ten tribes to the north of the Promised Land (Israel) lasted about 208 years after Solomon's death. The two southern tribes (Judah) lasted about 345 years. During all of those years other prophets like Elijah and Elijah tried to get Israel's kings and people spiritually back on track with their covenant with God. A number of prophets were sent by God to warn them of impending disaster if they did not change their ways. The Old Testament contains 17 books of the prophets. They all contain words of warning about the consequences of Israel's sins. Many of them also prophesied about the forthcoming victor over sin who was Jesus.

5. In the following passages from four of the prophetic books note the charges made against Israel by these prophets. What were some of the consequences of their sins? (Continued on the next page.)

Passages	Charges Against Israel	Consequences
Hosea 4:12-14		
Amos 5:21-27		
Micah 7:2-6		
Isaiah 1:1-7		

6. Based on the following verses from Micah 1:3-9 what judgments from God were to fall upon Israel?

Verses	Judgments
6	
7	
8	
9	

7. According to the following passages from Amos answer the questions.

Passages	Questions	Answers
7:10-13	What was Amos accused of by Amaziah?	
9:10	What was Israel's attitude toward these warnings from the prophets?	

8. God's appointed prophets had to compete with false prophets. Notice in Jeremiah 5:30-31 what the attitude of the people was toward the false prophets.

_____

_____

9. Even the great temple built by Solomon for God was desecrated. It too would not escape the pending destruction if Israel remained in their sinful ways. Read Jeremiah 7:1-11 and describe the prevailing spiritual conditions.

_____

_____

Note: The arrogance of the Israelites got the best of them. They thought surely God would not destroy Jerusalem because the temple was there. They acted like the temple was their good luck charm.

10. Read Jonah 1 and 2. Some prophecy was successful as it had its intended effect, one example being found in Jonah 3. According to the following verses from Jonah 3 note the events.

Verses	Events
1-2	
3-4	
5-9	
10	

11. Israel too could have avoided destruction if they truly repented. But, they were deaf to the warnings of the prophets. Justice was dealt first to the northern ten tribes (Israel) and then in the two southern tribes (Judah).
(A) Based on 2 Kings 15:29 what happened to the much of the northern kingdom of Israel? _____

_____

(B) Based on 2 Kings 17:1-6 what happened to the rest of the northern tribes?

_____

_____

(C) Based on 2 Kings 25:21-22 what happened to the southern tribes?

_____

_____

(D) Based on 2 Kings 25:9-12 what happened to Jerusalem?_____

_____

_____

Note: The blessing of the Promised Land was lost. But hope remained among many Israelites that some day they would be restored.

Session 17 Discussion Questions

1. Elijah was one of many prophets God raised up to awaken Israel out of their spiritual sleep. Does God raise-up prophets today to awaked people from their disbelief?

2. Most of the 40 kings after Solomon were not faithful to God. Prophets like Elijah and Elijah tried to get Israel's kings and people spiritually back on track with their covenant with God. A number of prophets were sent by God to warn them of impending disaster if they did not change their ways. How are we to heed the same warnings today?

3. What were some of the consequences of sins committed today?

4. Jonah prophesied to the people of Nineveh, warning them of pending disaster if they did not turn back to God. The people of Nineveh repented. As a result God showed compassion and forgave the people. He saved them from destruction. How does this apply to people today?

Suggested Reading for Session 18

1 Chronicles, 2 Chronicles, and Lamentations

Progress:

GELNDJJR1S2S1K2K1C2CENEJPPESIJLEDHJAOJMNHZHZM-MMLJAR1C2CGEPC1T2T1T2TTPHJ1P2P1J2J3JJR

The Exile – Session 18

Opening Prayer

Lord God your statutes are wonderful. Therefore we desire to obey them. The unfolding of your words gives us light and understanding. We long for your commands. Turn to us and have mercy on us as you do for all of those who love your name. Direct our footsteps according to your Word and let no sin rule over us. Guide us in this study that we may learn your truths. In Jesus's name we pray. Amen (Psalm 119)

Introduction

In the last session we reviewed key events from both Elijah and Elisha's ministries. Further, we reviewed some of the warnings to the Israelites from other prophets. They warned that if Israel did not change and come back to the true God they would be punished. Israel was defeated, destroyed, and many of the Israelites were carried off into captivity to foreign lands. Israel did not heed the warnings and God allowed all of this to happen. In this session we will review some other events before the captivity took place.

Session Material

Note: In this session we will step back to review both of the books of Chronicles. Bible experts suggest that Ezra wrote both books. These books contain fairly detailed accounts of events from Israel's history. They read like a history book with events presented pretty much in chronological order. For the most part just the historical facts are presented. Most of the history recorded in the books of Chronicles took place during the reigns of King David and King Solomon. The books of Kings focused mainly on both the northern and southern tribes. The books of Chronicles focus on David and the southern tribes in Judah.

1. The first nine chapters of 1 Chronicles details the genealogies of many of Israel's leaders. Based on the following passages from 1 Chronicles, record the names of the key leaders that are mentioned. (Continued on the next page.)

Passages	Key Leaders
1:1	
1:3	
1:4	
1:28	
2:1	
3:1	
3:5	

8:33	

2. These and other leaders mentioned provide a list of real people and real history for the Israelite people; not just a collection of unrelated legends. From that list of leaders would eventually come the real king, Jesus Christ. According to Romans 1:1-3 from whose family line did Jesus come? _____

3. The rest of 1 Chronicles, chapters 10-29, focus on David's kingship. Based on the following passages from 1 Chronicles what key events are mentioned?

Passages	David's Key Events
11:3	
11:4	
14:16-17	
15:3	
17:11-14	
28:9-11	

4. The first 7 chapters of 2 Chronicles records Solomon's leadership in the building of the temple in Jerusalem. Up to this point God had dwelt in a tabernacle which was a tent. For about 400 years they worshiped God in a tent, beginning right after the exodus from Egypt. Now it was time for a permanent temple building to be built. Based on 1 Chronicles 22:5 describe David's instructions about what the temple was to be like. _____

_____

5. The temple took about 7 years to build and it lasted about 375 years. In 586 B.C. the temple was destroyed by the Babylonian army because Israel refused to obey God. Read 2 Chronicles 7:19-22. According to verse 20 what three things did God warn Solomon that he would do?

(1) _____.

(2) _____.

(3) _____.

6. According to the following verses from 2 Chronicles 36, answer the following questions. (Continued on the next page.)

Verses	Questions	Answers
15	Who did God send to the Israelites to teach and warn them?	
16a	What was the attitude of the people toward God and the messengers?	

16b	As a result what was God's attitude toward the Israelites?	
17-19	What happened to the Israelites and the temple?	
20-21	What happened to some of the Israelites?	

Note: Instead of totally eliminating his chosen people, many were spared but were forced to live in bondage under the pagan king, Nebuchadnezzar. The remaining Israelites remained hopeful that Israel would one day be restored because of the promise God made to David about an everlasting throne.

7. It was most likely Jeremiah, the prophet, who described the fall of Jerusalem in the book of Lamentations. Read Lamentations 1:1-3 and describe the lament (or grief) shown by the author. _____

_____

8. Based on the following verses from Lamentations 2 describe God's attitude toward the Israelites because of their sin.

Verses	God's Judgments
2	
3	
4	
17	

9. Read Lamentations 3:41-45 and describe what happened. _____

_____

10. What message of hope is hinted in Lamentations 4:22? _____

_____

Note: A remnant of the Israelite people would be saved to fulfill the covenant promise made that David's kingdom would live forever. God's chosen people would be restored to fulfill the promised blessing that all people on earth would be blessed through them.

11. Hope for restoration had come from the prophets but their words had been ignored. What hope was given based on the following passages from these prophets? (Continued on the next page.)

Passages	Words of Hope
Isaiah 1:25-27	
Jeremiah 24:1-7	
Ezekiel 43:6-9	

12. Based on Jeremiah 29:10 how long <u>would</u> Israel live in bondage? _____
Based on 2 Chronicles 36:21 how long <u>did</u> Israel live in bondage? _____

Session 18 Discussion Questions

1. God's people mocked God's messengers, despised their words, and scoffed at the prophets. As a result God's wrath was so great that there was no remedy for their sins. How does the same thing happen today?

2. Because of his anger, God cut off his people. He treated them like an enemy or foe. He did what he planned to do if the people were unfaithful. He showed no pity. We too will be destroyed if we do not remain faithful. What can happen?

3. The Israelites prayers did not get through to God because of his anger toward them. They had gone too far into sin and God refused to listen to them. In what ways can we demonstrate our faithfulness to God based on the following four categories?

- Time

- Talents

- Tithes

- Testimony

Suggested Reading for Session 19

Ezra, Nehemiah, Esther

Progress:

GELNDJJR1S2S1K2K1C2CENEJPPESIJLEDHJAOJMNHZHZMM-MLJAR1C2CGEPC1T2T1T2TTPHJ1P2P1J2J3JJR

The Restoration – Session 19

Opening Prayer

Lord God we are full of joy because your love surrounds the whole earth. We gladly worship you because we know you made us and therefore we are yours. You watch over us. You are a great Lord. Your love endures forever. Your faithfulness continues through all generations. Help us in our Bible studies so that we can more fully know you. In Jesus's name we pray. Amen (Psalm 100)

Introduction

In the last session we reviewed some of the key people and events of Israel's history as they were documented in both books of Chronicles. We also reviewed some of the main points in the book of Lamentations. In that book we saw the grief experienced by the survivors, the remnant, of the Israelites while in captivity some 500 miles from their homeland. In this session we will see how God allowed Israel to be somewhat restored back in the Promised Land.

Session Material

Note: From the dates and events below we can see how God arranged international events that would enable a remnant of the Israelites to return to their homeland:

- 586 BC - Jerusalem was the last part of the Promised Land to be conquered by King Nebuchadnezzar of Babylon.
- 562 BC - King Nebuchadnezzar died.
- 539 BC - Persia conquered Babylon and they freed the Israelites.

1. The next three books in the Bible, i.e., Ezra, Nehemiah, and Esther; provide the rest of the Old Testament story. Israel had experienced the lowest point in its history. Now the future appeared promising because there was hope for restoration. Read Ezra 1:1-7 and note who God used to help begin the restoration process.

_____

2. Based on Ezra 7:6 and 10 describe Ezra's leadership skills. _____

_____

3. According to the following passages, answer the questions. (Continued on the next page.)

Passages	Questions	Answers
Ezra 2:64	About how many people were in the first group to go back to Jerusalem?	

Ezra 1:3	What was their top priority?	
Ezra 3:8	Who was their leader?	
Matthew 1:12 (Luke 3:27)	What was significant about him?	

4. (A) List the key events recorded in the following passages. Notice how God is at work in them.

Passages	Key Events
Isaiah 44:26-28 and 45:1 & 13	
Daniel 3	
Daniel 5	
Daniel 6	
Ezra 1:2	

(B) Why you think King Cyrus was so friendly and helpful toward the Israelites?

_____

_____

5. The second group of Israelites who returned to Jerusalem was led by Ezra in about 458 BC. About 1754 men, many women, and children accompanied him. According to Ezra 9:1-4 what greatly disturbed him when he got there? _____

_____

6. The Israelites repented and based on Ezra 10:1-3 what did they do? _____

_____

7. (A) About 26 years later another leader, Nehemiah, arrived in Jerusalem. What position did he hold in Jerusalem according to Nehemiah 8:9? _____

(B) What would become his top priority according to Nehemiah 1:2-4? _____

_____

8. Based on the following passages from Nehemiah how did the Israelites demonstrate their thankfulness to God for their restoration in Jerusalem? (Continued on the next page.)

Passages	Thankful Actions
8:18	
9:1	
9:2	
9:3	
10:29	
10:37	

9. Even though Israel had been released from bondage there were still enemies to be found. God intervened again with his chosen people. Based on the following passages from the book of Esther, answer the questions.

Passages	Questions	Answers
1:19	Who was king of Persia?	
2:5-7	Who raised Esther?	
2:10	What was Esther's nationality?	
2:17	Who became queen of Persia?	
3:8-10	What did Haman want to do?	
7:1-4	What did Esther do?	
8:7-11	What was the result?	

10. Based on Esther 1:1 how vast was the Persian Empire? _____

_____

11. The five books that follow Esther are referred to as the books of poetry. Name the books and who wrote them?

Book Name	Author

Session 19 Discussion Questions

1. In this session we saw how God arranged international events that would enable the remnant of the Israelites to return to their homeland. In what ways does God orchestrate international events today?

2. King Cyrus remembered the following key events:
   a. Shadrach, Meshach, and Abednego survived the fiery furnace.
   b. Daniel interpreted the king's dream; that the Medes and Persians would defeat Babylonia.
   c. Daniel survived the lions' den.

And, after receiving directions from God, King Cyrus let Israelites go back to their homeland. He respected the God who controls all of life's events. What is the colossal message in those events that we today would be well to remember?

3. Those returning from the exile did not remain faithful. They intermarried with nonbelievers. God was concerned that non-believing spouses would lead them away from faith in God. Does this apply today? If yes, how?

Suggested Reading for Session 20

Job
Review the 17 prophetic books again beginning with Isaiah and ending with Malachi. Become familiar with who these Old Testament prophets were.

Progress:

GELNDJJR1S2S1K2K1C2CENEJPPESIJLEDHJAOJMNHZHZM-MMLJAR1C2CGEPC1T2T1T2TTPHJ1P2P1J2J3JJR

Job and the Prophets – Session 20

<u>**Opening Prayer**</u>

Lord God help us realize that your discipline is really for our good although it may not seem like it at the time. In our study of your Word help us grow in the knowledge and wisdom of your laws and decrees. Grant us relief from days of trouble. We thank you for not rejecting your faithful people when we fall shout of your will. Be with us as we study your word. In Jesus's name we pray. Amen (Psalm 94)

<u>**Introduction**</u>

In the last session we studied the various events planned by God to restore his chosen people back into the Promised Land. God used Ezra the priest, Nehemiah the governor, and Esther the Persian queen to help restore and rebuild their nation. The nation was now much smaller but just as important as ever. In this session we will review the book of Job and the books of the prophets.

<u>**Session Material**</u>

1. The book of Job debates at great length the question of why misfortune happens to righteous people. Based on the following verses from Job 1, answer the questions.

Verses	Questions	Answers
1	Was Job a God fearing man?	
2	How many children did he have?	
3	How wealthy was Job?	

Note: Job lived in Edom (southeast of the Dead Sea.) some time after the reign of King Solomon.

2. Job had it all. But, God allowed his faith to be tested in some very difficult ways. According to the following verses from Job 1, summarize the events that happened to Job.

Verses	Events faced by Job
13-15	
16	
17	
18-19	

3. Nevertheless what was Job's response to these events according to Job 1:20-22? _____

_____

4. (A) After losing almost everything he had, what else went wrong with Job based on Job 2:7-8? _____

(B) Based on verse 9 what was Job's wife's advice? _____

_____

(C) According to verse 10 how did Job respond to his wife's advice? _____

_____

5. God allows suffering and troubles to occur to his faithful followers because of punishment for sin; test of faith as in Job's case; and discipline to help grow our faith. According to 1 Thessalonians 5:16-18 what are we to do when things don't go our way? _____

_____

6. According to the following passages from Job what other lessons can we learn from Job that are relevant to us today?

Passages	Other Lessons for Today
5:17	
19:25-27	

7. According to the following verses from Job 42 summarize how God blessed Job because of his faithfulness.

Verses	Job's Blessings
10	
11	
12	
13	
16	

Note: The rest of the books in the Old Testament are comprised of the 17 books from the 16 prophets. (The book of Lamentations is not usually considered to be a book of prophecy.) Each of these prophets was called by God to be his mouthpiece to the kings and to the people of their day. See Deuteronomy 18:18-19. The period of these prophets started with Elijah and Elisha, and lasted for about 445 years through the period of the kings. Some of the prophets foretold events that would be fulfilled within a short time period. For example, Daniel's prophecy that King Belshazzar would be killed and his kingdom would be conquered by the Medes and Persians (Daniel 5:25-31) all happened within a few days. Some prophecies were fulfilled within a couple of decades. Still other prophecies were made about events far into our future.

8. According to the following verses from Deuteronomy 18 answer these questions about prophets.

Verses	Questions	Answers
20	What was to happen to false prophets?	
21-22	How are we to know if a prophet is from God?	

9. There are at least five types or groups of prophecies that the prophets made. The following examples provide a sample of each type.

(1) The first group of prophecies foretell of the punishment that would be inflicted on Israel's neighboring nations because of their sins. Based on the following passages from Amos list the nations that would see God's judgment?

Passages	Nations
1:5	
1:8	
1:9-10	
1:11	
1:13-15	
2:1-2	

(2) The second group of prophecies dealt with Judah and Israel's fall because of their sin. According to Habakkuk1:2-6 what was Habakkuk's complaint and what was God's response?
Habakkuk's complaint: _____
God's response:_____

Note: Hosea also foretold the break-up of Israel and that Assyria would rule over them. See Hosea 8:14, 9:3, 9:17, and 11:5.

(3) The third group of prophecies provided hope, that Judah would be restored. According to Joel 3:17-21 what did Joel foretell?_____

Note: Other prophets also foretold of these events, e.g., Jeremiah 29:10-14; Ezekiel 11:16-20; and Isaiah 1:25-27.

(4) The fourth group of prophecies were concerned with the coming of the Messiah. According to Isaiah 9:6-7 what did Isaiah foretell some 700 years before it actually happened?_____

Note: Read Isaiah 52:13 through 53:12 to see the vivid details Isaiah foretold about our Suffering Servant, Jesus.

(5) The fifth group of prophecies foretells the events leading up to and including Christ's return to establish the new heaven and new earth. Read Daniel 12:1-4 and describe what major event will occur.

_____

_____

10. Who are two other important prophets found in the New Testament based on these clues?
A. He wrote the book of Revelation _____
B. He spoke the prophecy is recorded in Matthew 24._____

Session 20 Discussion Questions

1. Job had it all. But, God allowed his faith to be tested in some very difficult ways. How does God tenderize our faith today?

2. How can suffering and troubles make us a stronger Christian?

3. When Job lost almost everything he was full of sorrow and grief. But he praised God and did not blame him. He praised the name of the Lord. Is this attitude applicable to us today?

4. When we listen to evangelists who prophecy today, how are we to know if a prophet is from God?

Suggested Reading for Session 21

Review the Old Testament prophets.

Progress:

GELNDJJR1S2S1K2K1C2CENEJPPESIJLEDHJAOJMNHZHZM-MMLJAR1C2CGEPC1T2T1T2TTPHJ1P2P1J2J3JJR

O. T. Review and Events between the Testaments – Session 21

Opening Prayer

Lord God we sing for joy to you because you are the rock of our salvation. We come to you with thanksgiving. Lord, you are the great King above all gods. You made the mountains, the seas, the dry land, and all living creatures. We bow down before you in awe and respect because you are our God and we are in your care. Through these Bible studies enlighten us with more knowledge of your greatness and wisdom in order that we will be more effective servants for you. In Jesus's name we pray. Amen (Psalm 95)

Introduction

In the last session we studied the book of Job and reviewed some of the books written by the 16 Old Testament prophets. Now we leave the Old Testament with the Jews back in Judah and most importantly in Jerusalem; but still under Persian rule. In this session we will do a brief review of how Israel got to this point in their history. We will summarize key events that occurred in the 400 or so years between the end of the Old Testament and the beginning of the New Testament. Further, we will review what some of the prophets foretold.

Session Material

1. Review the following key events in Israel's (our) history and their approximate dates. Some names are missing in the grey boxes. Fill in the names based on the clues that are provided in the "Notes" column. (Continued on the next page.)

Dates B.C.	People	Notes
4000	Adam and Eve	They were the first created humans.
3000		He and his family survived the flood.
2166-1991		Covenant established with God. First son was Ishmael.
2066-1886	Isaac	Almost sacrificed by Abraham.
2006-1856		Father of the 12 Tribes, his name was changed to Israel.
1915-1805		He was a slave but he rose to become the number two leader of all of Egypt.
1876-1446	Israelites	In Egypt 450 years, became slaves.
1526-1406		God used him to facilitate the ten plagues on Egypt, journey to the Promised Land.
1375-1050	15 Judges	Samuel was the last judge.
1050-1010		Israel's first king started strong but had a weak finish.

Dates	People	Notes
1010-970	King David	He was promised an everlasting throne by God. He defeated all of the surrounding pagan nations.
970-930		He was king during Israel's peak of prosperity as a nation.
930-586 16 Prophets	20 Northern Kings-Israel and 20 Southern Kings-Judah	After Solomon's reign, Israel split in two. In 722 Assyria conquered Northern Kingdom. In 612 Babylon conquered Assyria. In 586 Jerusalem (Southern Kingdom) is conquered by Babylon.
539	Israelites	Persia conquered Babylon.
538	Zerubbel	Group 1 returned to Jerusalem.
516	Israelites	Temple was rebuilt. Period of Confucius and Buddha.
473		She helped save the Jews from massacre by because she was a Queen.
458	Ezra	Group 2 returns to Jerusalem.
432	Nehemiah	Group 3 returns to Jerusalem.
539-330	----------	Persian period of rule.
330-167	----------	Greek period of rule and Hellenism spreads.
167-63	----------	Maccabean period.
63 B.C-onward	----------	Roman period.
Dates	**People**	**Notes**
B.C. 5		The approximate date the Savior was born.
A.D. 26	Jesus	The approximate date he was baptized.
A.D. 28	Jesus	The approximate date he was crucified.
A.D. 35		He was a Jew but he converted to Christianity
A.D. 95	John	He wrote the book of Revelation.

Note: Israel never did regain national prominence as they had experienced under Kings David and Solomon. In fact, Israel generally existed as a vassal state to other more powerful nations.

Note: Three major power shifts occurred between the Old and New Testaments. In about 330 B.C. the Persian Empire was conquered by Alexander the Great, ending Persia's 200 year reign. Alexander, commander of the Greek army, conquered the lands of Egypt, Assyria, Babylon, and Persia over a period of about five years. Alexander was determined to change the world to a common language (Greek) and a common culture referred to as Hellenism. After Alexander's death his generals continued in his footsteps for about 163 years. They were tough on the Jews. At one point they even attempted to eradicate the Jewish religion. This caused some Jews who were led by Judas the Maccabee, to revolt and actually win Jewish independence for about 100 years. But then the Roman Empire invaded Judea, the Promised Land, in 63 BC. Rome remained in power throughout the region all through the New Testament period.

2. With a war-torn history, a future that could see nothing but Roman rule, and a longing to return to a united Israel nation like in the glorious days of King Solomon; there was a deep want and desire for God to provide a king that would restore Israel's greatness. Note the prophecies found in the following passages.

Passages	Prophecies
Genesis 3:14-15	
Numbers 24:17-19	
Deuteronomy 18:15	
2 Samuel 7:16	
1 Kings 9:5	
Psalm 2	
Psalm 16:9-11	
Psalm 22:1, 16, 18	
Psalm 89:3-4, 27-29	
Isaiah 7:14	
Isaiah 9:6-7	
Jeremiah 23:5-6	
Ezekiel 37:24-28	
Micah 5:2-5	
Zechariah 9:9	

3. Would Israel to get the king they were looking for?_____

_____

_____

Note: This list of Old Testament Bible passages provide a sample of the prophecies about the coming King, Prince of Peace, God's First Born, Wonderful, and many other names used to describe Jesus' majesty and glory. These prophecies were made many centuries before they actually came true by men from different backgrounds over a period of about 450 years. According to God's own timetable his Son was to enter into the world and the world would never be the same. The major turning point in all of history started with Jesus' birth.

Session 21 Discussion Questions

1. Why is it a good idea to study the Old Testament books of the prophets?

2. So many times did the Israelites wander from God's laws and statutes. The consequence of it all was a crushed nation. It would never to be the same. How can a pagan nation today regain its prosperity?

3. Kingdoms come and they go. Egypt, Israel, Babylon, Assyria, Persia, Greece, Rome and many others over recorded history have lost their standing as the most powerful nation in the world. How can the United States lose its position as the world leader?

Suggested Reading for Session 22

Matthew 1-2 and Luke 1-3

Progress:

GELNDJJR1S2S1K2K1C2CENEJPPESIJLEDHJAOJMNHZHZM-MMLJAR1C2CGEPC1T2T1T2TTPHJ1P2P1J2J3JJR

Unto us a Savior is Born – Session 22

Opening Prayer

Lord God, the world started anew when your Son, Jesus, arrived. There was hope and anticipation that the world would be a better place. But, sin had its way. You provided a plan of salvation through the sacrifice of your Son. Through these studies help us grow even closer to you and your will for our lives. Help us do this only for your glory. In Jesus's name we pray. Amen

Introduction

In the last session we reviewed many of the key events and people from the Old Testament. We then reviewed the four main national power shifts that occurred over the approximate 450 years from Ezra and Nehemiah to Jesus' birth; from Persian, to Greek, to Maccabean, and then to Roman supremacy. We also reviewed a sample of the prophecies about the promised Messiah. In this session we see that the promised Messiah arrives just as promised by the prophets many centuries earlier.

Session Material

1. As we begin our study of the New Testament we find that the first four books are: _____ , _____ , _____ , and _____ . They are referred to as the four Gospels. The word gospel means "good news". Each of these four books record key events from the Messiah's birth, his life, his tragic death, his resurrection, and his ascension. Messiah means "expected king and deliverer" of the Jews from the oppression that they had to endure for most of the years since the time of King Solomon, some 900 years earlier.

Note: From these four Gospels we see that many of the same events are recorded in more than one book. In fact many events are recorded in all four books. Even though these books have their own author they all guided by God to proclaim the same message: "God so loved the world that he gave his only Son and whoever believes in him will have everlasting life" (John 3:16). Each of the four books, however, was written from a different perspective, thus giving us a richer, fuller awareness of the Messiah and his ministry. What the Messiah said and did changed the world forever.

2. According to Galatians 4:4-7 when the time had fully come and when the world was just right, what did God do?_____

_____

3. (A) Review the genealogy found in Matthew 1:1-16 and note the familiar names in that list. Based on verse 16 whose genealogy is this? _____ .

(B) Now, review the genealogy found in Luke 3:23-38 and note the familiar names in this list too. According to verse 38 this genealogy begins with _____ and _____ . It traces Mary's ancestry all the way back to the beginning of time, showing Jesus' relationship to all of mankind.

4. **Jesus's Conception:** Details of the conception of the promised Messiah are recorded in both Matthew and Luke. Read Luke 1:26-38. According to the following verses answer the questions.

Verses	Questions	Answers
26	Who visited Mary?	
31	What was Mary told here?	
35	What was Mary told here?	
38	What was Mary's response?	

5. Mary was betrothed (engaged) to Joseph. Read Matthew 1:18-25. According to the following verses answer the questions.

Verses	Questions	Answers
19	After hearing of Mary's pregnancy, what was Joseph inclined to do?	
20-21	Who convinced him to do otherwise?	
22-23	Which prophet foretold this event?	
24-25	What was Joseph's response?	

6. **Jesus's Birth:** Details of Jesus's birth are recorded in Matthew and Luke. Read Luke 2:4-23. According to the following verses answer the questions. (Continued on the next page.)

Verses	Questions	Answers
4	What town was Jesus born in?	
7	Why was Jesus laid into a manger?	
8-16	Who first came to see Jesus?	

17-18 & 20	What was their response?	
19	What was Mary's response?	
21	On Jesus's eighth day what happened?	
22-24	On Jesus's 40th day what happened?	

7. Baby Jesus had other visitors. According to the following verses from Matthew 2 answer these questions.

Verses	Questions	Answers
1-2	Who came from the East to see Jesus?	
3-4	Why was King Herod and "all" Jerusalem disturbed?	
5-6	Which prophet foretold Jesus' birth in Bethlehem?	
11	When the visitors came to see Mary and Jesus, where were they staying?	
11-12	What three things did the visitors do?	1. 2. 3.

Note: In the whole history of the world there is a very short list of really important events that each one of us need to believe. (1) God created this world. (2) God saved this world through his Son, Jesus. (3) The day we come to believe it. (4) The day when Jesus returns to establish a new heaven and earth.

Session 22 Discussion Questions

1. Mary willingly accepted her assignment and went on to be a faithful servant. How does she provide an excellent role model for us?

2. There was no room for Joseph and Mary at the inn. If the innkeeper only knew who it was that they turned away. How can we make room for Jesus in our lives?

3. The shepherds spread the news, and the people were amazed. They also praised and glorified God. How can we spread the good news and glorify God?

Suggested Reading for Session 23

Matthew 3-13 and Luke 4

Progress:

GELNDJJR1S2S1K2K1C2CENEJPPESIJLEDHJAOJMNHZHZM-MMLJAR1C2CGEPC1T2T1T2TTPHJ1P2P1J2J3JJR

Jesus's Childhood and Early Ministry – Session 23

Opening Prayer

Lord God, you have been our dwelling place, our rock, and fortress throughout all generations. Before the mountains you were born. You have always been. You brought forth the earth and everything in it. From everlasting to everlasting you are God. You brought forth your Son so that we can have everlasting life with you. Bless us in our study of your Word so that we may apply it and be found worthy of your gift of everlasting life. In Jesus's name we pray. Amen (Psalm 90)

Introduction

In the last session we began to study the four Gospels: Matthew, Mark, Luke, and John. We reviewed the details about Jesus's conception and his birth. We also discussed baby Jesus's visitors: the shepherds and the Magi. In this session we will study Jesus's childhood and the beginning of his ministry.

Session Material

1. Jesus's Childhood: In the last session we discussed the fact that King Herod and all of Jerusalem were disturbed over the birth of Jesus because it had been prophesied that he would become the king of the Jews. Jesus was in danger because of King Herod's jealousy and fear. Based on the following verses from Matthew 2, answer these questions.

Verses	Questions	Answers
13-14	Who warned Joseph to escape to Egypt?	
15	Who was the prophet referenced in this verse?	
16	What evil action did King Herod order?	
17-18	Which prophet foretold this event?	
19-23	After the king died where did the angel tell Joseph take his family to live?	

Note: Many details of Jesus's life were foretold by the prophets of the Old Testament. The Bible records some 300 prophecies of Jesus's life and all were fulfilled. Joseph and his family lived in Egypt for about two years.

2. The Bible is silent about the next ten years of Jesus's childhood except Luke 2:39-40 mentions that he grew up in Nazareth and became strong. He was filled

with wisdom and God's grace was upon him. Read Luke 2:41-52. Here we find Jesus is 12 years old. According to the following verses from Luke 2 answer these questions.

Verses	Questions	Answers
49-50	At 12 years old what profound announcement does Jesus make to his parents?	
48 & 50	What was Jesus's parent's reaction to what he was doing and what he said?	
51	What personality characteristic of Jesus is mentioned?	
52	In what other ways did Jesus grow up?	

Note: Verses 46 and 52 indicates that Jesus was not all knowing (omniscient) or full of wisdom from his birth. The verse mentions that he grew up almost like any other boy.

3. Read Matthew 13:54-56 and note other details about Jesus' family.

(A) Jesus' hometown was _____.

(B) Jesus dad was a _____.

(C) Jesus had _____ brothers.

(D) Jesus had _____ sisters.

4. Another very important person was born about six months before Jesus. Answer these questions based on the following verses from Luke 1.

Verses	Questions	Answers
11-15	What was promised to Zechariah and Elizabeth?	
19	Who told Zechariah about this?	
16-17	What was John's mission to be?	- -

Note: Like the prophet Elijah, verse 17 mentions that John also was bold and faithful. Isaiah 40:3 foretells of a man who would be "a voice of one calling in the desert prepare the way for the Lord..." This was foretold some 700 years before John's birth.

5. Read John 1:19-27. According to the following verses, what key points does John make to the priests and Levites?

Verses	Key Points
20	
23	

6. **Jesus as a Young Man:** Based on the following verses from Luke 3, answer the following questions.

Verses	Questions	Answers
21	Who did John baptize?	
22	Whose voice did they hear?	
23	How old was Jesus when this occurred?	

7. Following Jesus' baptism the Holy Spirit led Jesus into the desert where he fasted for 40 days and was then tempted by the devil. According to the following verses from Matthew 4, in what ways was Jesus tempted by the devil and what were his responses?

Verses	Temptation	Other Bible References	Jesus's Responses
1-4		Deuteronomy 8:3	
5-7		Deuteronomy 6:16	
8-10		Deuteronomy 6:13-15	

8. **Jesus's Ministry Begins:** Read Matthew 4:12-17. After his baptism and desert temptations Jesus's formal ministry began as foretold by Isaiah. According to the following passages what was Jesus's ministry like? (Continued on the next page.)

Passages	Jesus's Ministry
2 Corinthians 8:9	
Luke 4:28-30	
Isaiah 53:3	
John 8:58-59	

Matthew 8:20	
Matthew:13:1-2	
Matthew 13:57	

Note: Jesus was very popular with many people and was hated by others. His message of hope and salvation upset the long held traditions of the synagogue. The Jewish leaders did not want to believe he was the Messiah. The political leaders did not want a new king that they feared would replace them. But the faithful people who were hurting, humbled, and in need of healing, sought him with fervor.

Session 23 Discussion Questions

1. At 12 years old Jesus wanted to be in the temple but his parents wanted him to go home with them. They did not fully understand who their son was. But God, with all things under his control, wanted his Son to obey his parents. How do we demonstrate our obedience to God in our daily walk with him?

2. Jesus grew in wisdom, stature and in favor with God. In what ways can we continue to grow regardless of our age?

3. Jesus met and defeated temptation with the truth found in God's Word. What truths from the Word help us resist temptation?

Suggested Reading for Session 24

Matthew 14-20 and Luke 5-15

Progress:

GELNDJJR1S2S1K2K1C2CENEJPPESIJLEDHJAOJMNHZHZM-MMLJAR1C2CGEPC1T2T1T2TTPHJ1P2P1J2J3JJR

Jesus Provides the Example – Session 24

Opening Prayer

Lord God, you reign over all. You are robed in majesty and are armed with strength. Your throne was established long ago from the beginning of eternity and will last for all of eternity. You are mightier than the thunder and mightier than the breakers of the sea. You alone are mighty. Your statutes stand firm and your holiness adorns your house forever. Help us with this study of your precious Word so we may continue to grow spiritually and grow closer to your will for our lives. In Jesus's name we pray. Amen (Psalm 93)

Introduction

In the last session we studied key points in Jesus's youth up to the beginning of his ministry when he was about 30 years old. We saw how some people hated him; some people ignored him; and many others sought and loved him. If he were alive today he probably would be received the same way. In this session we will continue to investigate various aspects of Jesus's ministry as they are recorded in the four Gospels.

Session Material

1. **Jesus the Leader:** Within a few days after his baptism Jesus began to form an important team to help him.
(A) Read John 1:38-44. What did Jesus do on this occasion? _____

_____

(B) Definition: A _____ is a person who accepts and promotes the teachings and doctrine of the leader. In this case Jesus was their leader.

2. Jesus's group of disciples grew.
(A) According to Luke 10:1 how many other disciples were there at this time?_____
(B) Read Luke 6:12-17. What did Jesus do on this occasion?

_____

(C) Definition: An _____ was a person commissioned by Jesus to preach and teach the Gospel and heal the sick. This special group of 12 leaders was selected from among the disciples. Paul, James, and Barnabas were added later.

3. According to Luke 9:1-6 how were the Apostles empowered and why?

How: _____

Why: _____

4. Based on John 6:53-71 did all of Jesus's disciples remain faithful? _____

5. Some months later Jesus commissioned a group of 72 disciples to go out in pairs to surrounding towns and villages. Based on Luke 10:17 how successful was this missionary effort? _____

Note: Jesus's goal was to develop a core group of missionaries, preachers, teachers, and healers upon which to build for the future. They learned from the Master himself. They heard his teachings first hand. They saw the miracles he performed. They saw how he handled many different situations as he applied his teachings to the humble and broken people that sought him. The Apostles were to become the first leaders of the Christian church as we know it today.

6. Not long after his baptism Jesus demonstrated courage when he stood up for his convictions. According to John 2:13-17 what did Jesus do?_____

7. **Jesus the Preacher:** Based on the following passages note how well Jesus' preaching was received.

Passages	Jesus's Preaching
Matthew 4:23-25	
Matthew 5:1 through 7:29	
Matthew 9:35-36	

8. When Jesus preached and taught he often used short stories to illustrate the point he was making. Definition: Jesus' _____ were short stories designed to emphasize a moral, religious or spiritual principle. There are about 35 of them recorded throughout the four Gospels.

9. The passages below provide three typical examples of parables spoken by Jesus. Note how Jesus used basic illustrations and ideas out of ordinary everyday life to promote interest and understanding to the point he was trying to make. The parables were used to illustrate important truths and teach important lessons to the people. Many of them are recorded in more than one of the four Gospels. Read the following parables and describe the important lesson that was given. (Continued on the next page.)

Passages	Important Lessons
Mark 4:2-8 & 14-20	

Luke 15:11-32	
Matthew 20:1-16	

10. **Jesus the Friend:** The Gospels record many examples of how Jesus befriended people. Note the outcomes of the friendships which are mentioned in the following passages.

Passages	Incident	Outcome
John 4:4-42	Jesus talked to the woman at Jacob's well.	
Luke 7:36-50	The sinful woman washes Jesus' feet.	
John 12:1-8	Jesus's friends give him a dinner in his honor. Mary put perfume on his feet.	
Mark 10:13-16	Jesus corrects the disciples about children.	
John 11:32-44	Jesus cries for his friends.	

Note: The great spiritual song written by Joseph Scriven reminds us about "What a Friend We Have in Jesus". He is our friend no matter what. In Scriven's words:
- Do we have trials and temptations?
- Are we weak and heavy laden?
- Do your friends despise-forsake us?
- Who will all our sorrows share?
- We should never be discouraged.
- Take it to the Lord in prayer.

Note: Before raising Lazarus form the grave Jesus prayed. Many other times the Scriptures record that Jesus prayed. In times of distress, hopelessness, frustration, and even in happy times it is important for us to pray whether it be for help or for thanks.

Session 24 Discussion Questions

1. Jesus demonstrated courage when he stood up for his convictions as he drove the merchants and money changers out of the temple. How can we demonstrate our courage for our convictions?

2. Based on John 6:53-71 not all of Jesus's disciples remain faithful. Some fell away. Apparently they were not ready to do what it takes to be a follower of Jesus. What does it take to be a follower of Jesus?

3. The parable of the lost son illustrates the patience the father (God) has for his errant children. God is always ready to receive believers back if they drift away from him. Is there any unforgivable sin?

Suggested Reading for Session 25

Matthew 21-28 and Luke 16-24

Progress:

GELNDJJR1S2S1K2K1C2CENEJPPESIJLEDHJAOJMNHZHZM-MMLJAR1C2CGEPC1T2T1T2TTPHJ1P2P1J2J3JJR

Jesus's Ministry – Session 25

Opening Prayer

Lord God, your Word is eternal. It stands firm in the heavens. Your faithfulness continues through all generations. You established the earth, and it endures. Your laws endure to this day for all things serve you. If your law had not been our delight we would have perished long ago. We will never forget your precepts for by them you preserve our lives. Help us to more deeply know, appreciate and live your Word. In Jesus's name we pray. Amen (Psalm 119)

Introduction

In the last session we studied details about Jesus as a leader, a preacher, and a friend. He formed a group of disciples, 12 of which were made apostles. We saw how he often used parables to teach the disciples and crowds. We saw how Jesus befriended people and how that friendship impacted them for the better. In this session we will study the remainder of Jesus' three-year ministry.

Session Material

1. **Jesus's Miracles:** There are four main groups of miracles that Jesus performed during his three-year ministry. The Gospels record 35 of his miracles. Many of them are recorded in more than one on the Gospels. The first group of miracles involved the healing of sickness and disease. A sample of these healings is found in the following passages. From each passage note who was healed and from what they were healed.

Passages	Who	What
Matthew 9:27-31		
Mark 2:3-12		
Luke 13:11-13		
John 4:47-53		

2. The second group of miracles performed by Jesus involved delivering people from demon possession. A sample of these healings is found in the following passages. From each passage note who was healed and from what they were healed.

Passages	Who	What
Matthew 17:14-18		
Mark 5:1-15		
Luke 4:33-37		

3. The third group of miracles performed by Jesus involved subduing nature in some way. A sample of these miracles is found in the following passages. What were the miracles?

Passages	Jesus's Miracles
Matthew 8:23-27	
Mark 6:47-51	
Luke 9:12-17	
John 2:1-11	

4. The forth group of miracles performed by Jesus demonstrated God's power over death. Based on the following passages who were brought back to life?

Passages	Who
Mark 5:22-24 & 38-42	
Luke 7:11-15	
John 11:1-44	

5. Jesus told many parables, preached many sermons, taught many principles and performed many miracles. Based on John 21:25 how many other events occurred that did not get written into the four Gospels?_____

_____

Note: Even though everything Jesus did was not recorded, enough has been written to capture the divine acts of love and sacrifice to show all people the plan of salvation that he provided. The Bible documents all we need to know to gain his blessed assurance of forgiveness and everlasting life so long as we believe in him.

6. According on John 20:31 what is the fundamental purpose of the parables and miracles that are documented in the four Gospels?_____

_____

7. **Jesus Our Sacrifice:** According to the following passages note the events of Jesus's last week. (Continued on the next page.)

Passages	Day	Events
John 12:12-17	Sunday	
Mark 11:15-18	Monday	
Matthew 21:23-27	Tuesday	

Luke 22:1-6	Wednesday	
Mark 14:12-25 & 43-46	Thursday	- -
Matthew 27:27-66	Friday	
Luke 24:1-12	Sunday	

8. **Jesus Our Resurrected Lord:** The following events prove that Jesus rose from the dead. He appeared to many people on many occasions. Many of these appearances of Jesus are recorded in more than one of the Gospels. According to the following passages, who actually saw Jesus after his death?

Passages	When	Who
John 20:10-18	Sunday	
Luke 24:13-35	Sunday	
Luke 24:36-43	Sunday	
John 20:26-29	Week Later	
John 21:1-24	Later	
Matthew 28:16-20	Later	
1 Corinthians 15:6	Later	
1 Corinthians 15:7	Later	
Acts 1:3-11 & Luke 23:50-52	40 days after resurrection – Jesus' ascension to heaven	

9. According to Isaiah 53:4-5 and John 1:29 why did Jesus go through the crucifixion and die as he did?_____

_____

_____

10. Where is Jesus now according to Ephesians 1:20-23? _____

_____

Note: Read Philippians 2:9-11 to better understand Christ's exaltation. He has and uses his divine powers as part of the Godhead. Revelation 1:7 tells us that Jesus will return to complete the final judgment by separating evil from good (2 Corinthians 5:10). Then he will establish a new heaven and a new earth according to 2 Peter 3:13.

Note: If you get engaged in a conversation about Jesus with an unsaved person, what do you gently need to tell them?

- Romans 3:10 - Nobody is righteous, not even one.
- Romans 3:22 – Righteousness from God comes through faith in Jesus Christ, for all who believe.
- Romans 3:23 - All of us have sinned and fallen short of God's glory.
- Romans 3:24 - We are justified freely by God's grace through the redemption that comes only by Jesus Christ.
- Romans 3:25 - God presented Jesus as a sacrifice of atonement through faith in his shed blood.
- John 3:16: God loved the world so much he gave his only Son, Jesus, to come to earth and die for our sins. Whoever believes in him will not die but will have everlasting life.

Have the person pray with you: Lord God:

- I confess that I am a sinner.
- I am sorry for my sins.
- With the help of the Holy Spirit:
  - I will change to be the person you want me to be.
  - Help me grow my faith in your Son, Jesus.
  - Help me grow my knowledge of your Word.
  - Give me a closer walk with You.
- Someday when my life's work is done, take me home to be with you.
- In Jesus's name I pray. Amen.

Session 25 Discussion Questions

1. Even though everything Jesus did during his ministry was not recorded, enough has been written to capture the divine acts of love and sacrifice to show all people for all time the plan of salvation he provided. The Bible documents all we need to know to gain his blessed assurance of forgiveness and everlasting life. What position do we need to take when someone mentions another book as having the truth about our faith?

2. How does someone who does not yet believe get saved?

3. If you get engaged in a conversation about Jesus with an unsaved person, some of the discussion you have with them in noted above. How should you follow-up with the new Christian?

Suggested Reading for Session 26

Acts 1-9 and 1 Peter 1-5

Progress:

GELNDJJR1S2S1K2K1C2CENEJPPESIJLEDHJAOJMNHZHZM-MMLJAR1C2CGEPC1T2T1T2TTPHJ1P2P1J2J3JJR

The Church Begins to Grow – Session 26

Opening Prayer

Lord God, we confess that we are sinners every day. Our thoughts, deeds and words are not always righteous and holy. Since our sin separates us from you we ask for your forgiveness. Help us, guide us and encourage us to live as we should. You are our light in this dark world. Have your Holy Spirit enlighten, motivate and guide us in the study of your Word. In Jesus's name we pray. Amen.

Introduction

In the last session we studied a sampling of Jesus' miracles. We reviewed key events during the week leading up to Jesus' crucifixion. We then studied a number of instances where people were visited by Jesus after his death; thus proving that his resurrection was real. In this session we will begin to see how Jesus's 3-year ministry changed the world's religious landscape forever.

Session Material

1. One of Jesus's main objectives was to establish his church here on earth. His church would be the driving force behind the command mentioned in Matthew 28:19-20. What was the command? _____

_____

2. Read Matthew 16:13-19. What message did Jesus give to his disciples?_____

_____

3. In Matthew 16:16 Peter confesses that Jesus was the Son of God. In verse 18 Jesus says that upon "this rock" I will build my church. According to the following passages who is the rock upon which the church is built?

Passages	Who is the Rock
Colossians 1:15-18	
Deuteronomy 32:3-4	
2 Samuel 22:2-3	
Psalm 19:14	
Psalm 92:14	
Isaiah 26:4	

4. Jesus intended for those first missionaries, his disciples, to spread the Gospel and grow his church. Even for us today, our role in the church is discussed in Romans 12:4-8. What is our role in Christ's church? _____

_____

5. The book of Acts was written by _____. Acts shows how the movement Jesus started during his 3-year ministry continued after his death and resurrection. The movement, i.e., the beginning of the Christian church, was accomplished through the efforts of the apostles and other new converts who were moved by God to do so. Acts reveals many key events and people during the first _____ years of the church.

6. Discuss the difference between what the disciples were looking for in Acts 1:6 and what Jesus had planned for them to do according to Acts 2:1-4. _____

_____

_____

7. Based on the following verses from Acts 2:42-47 what were the conditions like within the early church?

Verses	The Early Church
42	
43	
44	
45	
46	
47	

8. According to Acts 5:12-16 how successful was the Apostles' ministry? _____

_____

_____

9. The success of the apostles' ministry was not well received by all. According to the following passages what kinds of persecution did the apostles have to deal with?

Passages	Persecution
Acts 5:17-20	
Acts 7:54-60	
Acts 8:1	
Acts 8:3	
Acts 9:1-2	

10. The focus of the first 12 chapters of Acts is mainly on Peter's efforts to help build the church. Peter's ministry mainly focused on the Jews while Paul's mainly

focused on the Gentiles. Peter was part of a select group of three of the apostles. According to Mark 9:2-4 who else was part of this select group?

_____

11. Peter served as the spokesman for the apostles. Right after they were filled with the Holy Spirit on Pentecost what did Peter do according to Acts 2:14-40?

_____

_____

12. According to Acts 4:5-14 what did Peter do that impressed the high priest and others? _____

13. Later in his ministry Peter wrote two letters to his faithful friends in the churches in Asia Minor. Based on the following passages from 1 Peter, what earnest advice did he give them?

Passages	Advice
1:14-15	
2:1-3	
2:13-15	
3:1	
3:7	
3:8	

14. In Peter's first letter he mentioned the persecution that the Christians were facing.
(A) According to these verses from 1 Peter 3, what did he instruct the people to do and why?

Verses	Peter's Instructions
13	
14	
15	
16	

(B) According to 1 Peter 4:12-14 what is the reward for doing these things?

_____

_____

Session 26 Discussion Questions

1. Peter was bold and courageous as he spoke the truth about Jesus. How is that an example for us to follow today?

2. What advice should we give our Christian friends and family about how to live according to their faith?

3. If we are ever faced with persecution for our faith, what good advice can you give to help survive through it?

Suggested Reading for Session 27

Acts 10-14, 2 Peter 1-3, and Galatians 1-6

Progress:

GELNDJJR1S2S1K2K1C2CENEJPPESIJLEDHJAOJMNHZHZM-MMLJAR1C2CGEPC1T2T1T2TTPHJ1P2P1J2J3JJR

The Church Continues to Grow – Session 27

Opening Prayer

Lord God, our very souls glorify you. We rejoice in the saving power of your Son, Jesus. We forever humble ourselves before you in thanksgiving and praise. You do great things for your faithful people. Your mercy extends to those who fear, love, honor and respect you throughout all generations. Fill us with the knowledge and power of your Word so we continue to draw closer to you through these Bible studies. In Jesus's name we pray. Amen. (Luke 1)

Introduction

In the last session we studied how the church got its start. On Pentecost (about seven weeks after Easter) the apostles were given spiritual gifts from God to go and make disciples in all nations. We reviewed several characteristics of the early church. The apostles' ministry was successful as many were coming to faith daily. But, the early Christians were heavily persecuted by nonbelievers. In Peter's first letter to the churches in Asia Minor he gave them advice on how to live peaceably in spite of the persecution they faced. In this session we will continue our study of Peter's ministry and then begin a study of Paul's ministry.

Session Material

1. In Peter's second letter to the believers in Asia Minor what does he warn them about according to 2 Peter 2:1-3? _____

_____

2. Peter describes the end of the world as we know it and then describes what lies beyond it. Note the key points Peter makes about this based on the following verses from 2 Peter 3. (Continued on the next page.)

Verses	Peter's Main Points
1-2	
3-4	
5-6	
8-9	
10	

11-12	
13-14	

3. At the same time Peter was working to grow the Christian church who was working to destroy it according to Acts 8:1-3?_____

4. According to the following verses from Acts 9 record the events that happened to Saul.

Verses	Key Events of Saul
1-6	
7-9	
10-19	
20-22	
23-25	
26-27	
28-30	

5. According to Acts 13:9 what else was Saul called? _____

6. Peter's ministry had been focused on the conversion of Jews to Christianity. However the events in Acts 10 changed the direction of Christian ministry for all time. According to Acts 10:10-48 what happened? _____

_____

Note: About a year or so after Peter wrote his second letter, he was martyred during the reign of Nero, the Roman emperor, in about A.D. 68.

7. **Paul's First Missionary Journey:** Paul's first of four missionary journeys began about 15 years after Jesus' death and resurrection. The church was growing fast but conditions were unstable due to the persecution faced by all who came to faith in Jesus. Acts 13-14 record the cities Paul and his companions visited in this first journey. They left from Antioch, Syria for about two years. According to Acts 11:26 what were the new believers called for the first time?

_____

8. Read Acts 13:42-52. After Paul had just completed preaching in Antioch, Galatia on the Sabbath how was he received by the:

Believers (Mostly Gentiles): _____

Nonbelievers (Mostly Jews): _____

9. In many towns visited by Paul he was received the same way, i.e., many Gentiles were happy and the Jews were angry. In Iconium what caused Paul to flee according to Acts 14:4-6? _____

_____

10. According to Acts 14:19-20 what happened to Paul in Lystera? _____

_____

11. Paul eventually retraced his steps back to Antioch, Syria. According to Acts 14:27-28 what did Paul do upon his return home? _____

_____

_____

12. Just after his return home Paul wrote a letter to the Gentile Christians in the religion of Galatia where he had just visited. He wanted to reaffirm sound doctrine about the law and the gospel. Based on the following passages from Galatians what concerns did Paul address?

Passages	Paul's Comments
1:6-7	
3:1-5	
3:10	
3:26	
5:3-6	

Note: The key message in Paul's letter to the Galatians is the foundational principle; that works will not save a person. Rather, the believer is justified without their own merit, or works, or the law. We are saved by our faith in Jesus Christ alone. But, faith without works is dead.

Session 27 Discussion Questions

1. The world was destroyed with a flood because of mankind's sin. Next time it will be destroyed by fire. Should we Christians be concerned about this?

2. God's creation was destroyed with a flood because of sin. Have we learned our lesson to not sin? Why or why not?

3. Saul's heavenly vision was enough to convince him Jesus was real. It was hard for all of the believers he had been trying to persecute to accept him. When we become aware of someone who is a new believer, how should we treat them?

Suggested Reading for Session 28

Acts 15-20, 1 Corinthians 1-16, 2 Corinthians 1-13, I Thessalonians 1-5

Progress:

GELNDJJR1S2S1K2K1C2CENEJPPESIJLEDHJAOJMNHZHZM-MMLJAR1C2CGEPC1T2T1T2TTPHJ1P2P1J2J3JJR

Paul's 2nd and 3rd Missionary Journeys – Session 28

Opening Prayer

Lord God, you reign over all. We pray that every nation will come to know your great and awesome name because you love justice and have established equity. We exalt you Lord and worship you because only you are holy. You spoke to the Israelites in a pillar of cloud long ago and you speak to us today through your written and spoken Word. Help us to learn, know, and apply your Word in our daily lives. In Jesus's name we pray. Amen. (Psalm 99)

Introduction

In the last session we studied main points from Peter's second letter to the believers in Asia Minor. Our focus then shifted toward Saul, also known as Paul. We reviewed Paul's conversion to Christianity and his first missionary journey to Galatia in Asia Minor. Later, Paul wrote a letter to the Galatians to reaffirm sound doctrine about law and gospel. In this session we will study Paul's second and third missionary journeys. We will see that the persecution Paul and other believers faced increased with time.

Session Material

1. **Paul's Second Missionary Journey:** According to Acts 15:36 and 16:1-5 what were Paul's travel plans as he began his second missionary trip? _____

_____

_____

Note: It was very important for Paul to visit the new churches because many nonbelievers were trying to tear them apart by undermining their faith with false teachings. The new believers were being persecuted in those towns as well as in Jerusalem. Paul's second trip covered about 2200 miles round trip.

2. Even though there was persecution the church forged ahead. According to the following verses from Acts 16 what key activities were occurring?

Verses	Key Activities
4	
5	

3. According to the following passages from the book of Acts note the towns Paul and his companions visited and the persecution they experienced during this second missionary trip. Note that no persecution is mentioned in the towns that he

revisited from his first journey. On this trip Paul traveled from Jerusalem, to Antioch, then onward to what we today know as central and western Turkey.

Passages	Towns	Persecution
16:6-8		
16:11-12 & 22-23		
17:1-5		
17:10-14		
17:16-17 & 32		
18:1, 5-6 & 17		
18:19-20		
18:22		

4. It was about 20 years after Jesus' death and resurrection that Paul completed his second missionary journey and wrote both of his letters to the Christians in Thessalonica. Recall the mob scenes mentioned above? Based on the following passages from 1 Thessalonians, record the main points that Paul makes to them.

Passages	Paul's Main Points
3:1-7	
4:1-12	
4:13-18	
5:12-19	

5. About a third of Paul's second letter to the Thessalonians deals with eschatology or the end of the world when Christ returns. Many did not believe it. Read 2 Thessalonians 2:1-15 and summarize Paul's teaching about this matter.

_____

_____

_____

6. **Paul's Third Missionary Journey:** In his third journey Paul revisited many of the same towns he and his companions visited in previous journeys.
(A) According to Acts 18:23 what was his main mission? _____

_____

_____

(B) According to the following passages from the book of Acts, what were some of the things Paul did?

Passages	Paul's Tactics
19:8	
19:11-12	
20:1-2	
20:18-20	

Note: Paul provided a great example. Even though he had been beaten and imprisoned more than once, his faith and determination remained solid in Jesus.

7. It was near the time of Paul's third missionary journey that he wrote two letters to the Christians in Corinth. Like today, there were so many distractions: false teaching, ignorance, jealousy, and persecution. Based on the following passages from 1 Corinthians, note the key issues that Paul addressed with them.

Passages	Issues Paul Addressed
3:1-3	
4:18-19	
5:1 & 9-11	
6:1,4 & 7-8	
7:1-40	
8:4	
11:20-22	
13:4-8	
14:12	
15:3-8	
15:42-44 & 52-54	
16:1-2	

8. In Paul's second letter to the Christians in Corinth he addressed more important matters of faith. According to the following passages from 2 Corinthians, note the main issues Paul addressed.

Passages	Issues Paul Addressed
2:5-10	
5:17	
6:14	
9:6-8	

Session 28 Discussion Questions

1. The Apostles provided rules for proper worship, doctrine, and behavior for the new Christian churches. They continued with a strong emphasis on evangelism, preaching and teaching the unbelievers. Where should churches today place strong emphasis?

2. Paul encouraged proper Christian behavior. What are proper Christian behaviors today?

3. Paul said that we are not to be yoked together with unbelievers. What does this really mean?

Suggested Reading for Session 29

Romans 1-16, Ephesians 1-6, Philippians 1-4, and Colossians 1-4

Progress:

GELNDJJR1S2S1K2K1C2CENEJPPESIJLEDHJAOJMNHZHZM-MMLJAR1C2CGEPC1T2T1T2TTPHJ1P2P1J2J3JJR

More of Paul's Letters to the Faithful – Session 29

Opening Prayer

Lord God, as far as the heavens are above the earth is how great your love is for those who believe in you. As far as the east is from the west is how far you have removed our sins from us. Thank you for your compassion on us undeserving sinners. Help us to grow our faith in you through the continued study of your Word. In Jesus's name we pray. Amen. (Psalm 103)

Introduction

In the last session we studied Paul's second and some of his third missionary journeys. His main mission was to grow and strengthen the churches. There were many distractions attempting to dilute Jesus' teachings. There were no catechisms, no Christian manuals, no instruction books about how a church should operate; or exactly what the believers were suppose to believe. Paul worked tirelessly to help them remain faithful to Jesus' teachings and grow their faith. In this session we will study more of Paul's letters to the various churches. Again, he continues to encourage and teach them.

Session Material

1. Paul lists the suffering he endured during his ministry up to this point in 2 Corinthians 11:23-28. According to the following verses from that passage summarize some of the things that happened to Paul.

Verses	Paul's Suffering
23	
24	
25	
26	
27	
28	

2. Around the time of Paul's third missionary journey, he wrote a letter to the believers in Rome. This occurred about 30 years after Jesus' death and resurrection. Martin Luther mentioned that every Christian should know this book word for word and by heart because of its abundance of basic knowledge that every Christian should know. Paul wrote this book to prepare the believers for his eventual visit. According to the following passages from Romans, what main

points are made by Paul?

Passages	Paul's Main Points to the Romans
1:16	
1:17	
3:23	
3:24-25	
5:8	
6:23	
8:28	
12:1-2	
12:4-8	
12:9-19	

3. (A) According to Acts 23:11 where did Jesus tell Paul that he needed to go?
_____

(B) According to Acts 27:1 where did Paul eventually go? _____

4. Acts 21:17 through 28:31 records the events that led to Paul's compliance to Jesus's directions to go to Rome. God set the following events into motion. According to the following passages from Acts what were some of the major events? (Continued on the next page.)

Passages	Major Events
21:27-40	
22:1 thru 23:11	
23:12-35	
24:1-27	
25:1-12	
25:13 - 26:32	

27:1-28:10	
28:11-30	

5. During his two years in Rome Paul wrote four letters. The first letter was written to the Christians in Ephesus. In this letter Paul continues to strengthen the church with his teachings from and about Jesus. Based on the following passages from Ephesians, note the main points Paul made.

Passages	Paul's Main Points to the Ephesians
1:4-8	
1:9-10	
2:8-9	
2:10	
4:3-6	
6:10-18	

6. The second letter Paul wrote while in Rome was to the Christians in Philippi. According to the following passages from Philippians note Paul's main points.

Passages	Paul's Main Points to the Philippians
1:27-30	
2:1-11	
3:12-14	

7. The third letter written by Paul during his two years in Rome was to the Christians in Colosse. According to the following verses from Colossians 2 note the main points made by Paul about the prevailing false teaching. (Continued on the next page.)

Verses	Paul's Main Points to the Colossians
16	
18	
23	

8. (A) Read Colossians 3:5-9 and count the number of behaviors Paul mentions all believers <u>must not do</u>. _____ Take note of what they are.

(B) Read Colossians 3:12-14 and count the number of behaviors Paul mentions all believers <u>must do</u>. _____ Take note of what they are.

9. Read Colossians 3:11 and 16-17 and summarize Paul's teaching about how believers are to treat one another. _____

_____

_____

10. Paul's fourth letter written during his two years in Rome was to Philemon, a believer living in Colosse. Read Philemon 8-21 and answer the following questions.

Verses	Questions	Answers
10	What was the slave's name?	
15	Why was the slave with Paul?	
16	Why did Paul call him a brother?	
17-18	How did Paul restore the slave's relationship with his master?	

Note: Paul willingly paid the price to repair the Slave's relationship with his master. We too are slaves to sin. But, Jesus paid the price to repair our relationship with our Master who is God Almighty.

Session 29 Discussion Questions

1. How do all things God work out for the good for those who love God?

2. Give examples of how love is shown by actions, not just words.

3. How are we to offer our bodies as living sacrifices as we do God's will? We need to do things that sometimes we would prefer not doing; for example:

4. Paul taught about how believers are to treat one another. What are some of the things Christians should avoid as they let their light shine?

Suggested Reading for Session 30

1 Timothy 1-6, 2 Timothy 1-4, Titus 1-3, and Hebrews 1-13.

Progress:

GELNDJJR1S2S1K2K1C2CENEJPPESIJLEDHJAOJMNHZHZM-MMLJAR1C2CGEPC1T2T1T2TTPHJ1P2P1J2J3JJR

Paul's Fourth Missionary Journey – Session 30

Opening Prayer

Lord, we ask that your Holy Spirit touch all who study your Word because your Word is truth. It is the very foundation of our faith. In it we build confidence that our faith will grow so that we can be of greater service to you. Thank you Lord for your patience with us because of our sinful ways. Continue to refresh and motivate us as we continue to dig deeper into your Word. In Jesus's name we pray. Amen.

Introduction

In the last session we reviewed some of the hardships Paul endured during his ministry. We also looked into Paul's letters to the Christians in Rome, Ephesus, Philippi, and Colosse. We also looked at his letter to Philemon. In each case he reminded them that salvation is obtained through faith in Christ Jesus. Paul encouraged the churches to remain faithful. However there were many people trying to undermine the faith of the new believers. In this session we will review Paul's fourth missionary journey and the rest of the books that he wrote.

Session Material

1. After Paul's two year imprisonment in Rome, he was set free. Evidence from historians suggests that he went on a fourth missionary journey that lasted for about _____ years. Leaving from _____ he traveled west to _____ . Then he traveled all the way back to _____ _____ to some of the same churches he had worked with in his second and third missionary journeys. Finally, he traveled back to _____. The length of this journey was about _____ miles in all. It was during this journey that Paul wrote his first letter to Timothy and a letter to Titus.

2. In Paul's first letter to Timothy in Ephesus, he emphasized many of the same doctrines he discussed in his earlier letter to the Ephesians. Timothy had been one of Paul's companions in an earlier missionary journey. According to the following passages from 1 Timothy, what main points are reinforced by Paul?

Passages	Paul's Main Points
1:15	
2:5-6	
3:1-13	
4:9-10	

Note: In chapters 4-6 of 1 Timothy Paul discusses many behaviors and attitudes that are appropriate and necessary for a healthy Christian life. This letter from Paul reads like a manual for proper Christian living. It is based on the teachings of Jesus.

3. Also during Paul's fourth missionary journey he wrote a letter to Titus who was a leader of the church on the island of Crete. Read the following verses from Titus 1 and summarize the tasks Paul gave to Titus.

Verses	Titus' Tasks
5	
10-11	
13-14	
15-16	

4. According to the following verses from Titus 2 to who were teachings to be made?

Verses	To Who?
2	
3-5	
6-8	
9	

Note: God's Word is for everyone. Slavery was mentioned because it was part of Roman culture. Slaves were to:
- Be subject to their master.
- Please their master.
- Not back-talk to their master.
- Not steal from their master.
- Be trustworthy.

To be sure masters had their list of obligations and responsibilities too.

5. What were the two important and "trustworthy" points mentioned by Paul in Titus 3:3-8?

Verses	Two Trustworthy Points
3-6	
7-8	

6. Paul or one of his peers wrote the letter to the Hebrew Christians. It was an important letter to the Jewish converts living in the Judea, Ammon, Edom, and Moab regions. According to the following passages from Hebrews, who was Christ superior to?

Passages	Christ is Superior to:
1:1-4	
3:1-4	
7:23-28	

Note: The Jewish high priest was able to forgive sins, but they were sinners too. They sacrificed "spotless" animals to gain God's forgiveness. Jesus was made perfect and was without sin. When he faced temptation he resisted. Jesus was always obedient to his Father. Therefore he was made perfect forever and was the perfect (spotless) sacrifice for all believers for all time for the forgiveness of sins.

7. Based on Hebrews 9:14-15 what was the important message given to the Hebrew believers?_____

_____

Note: To the believing Jews, no longer were animal sacrifices needed. Jesus was the perfect sacrifice. Note the reoccurring messages in each of Paul's letters:
- Jesus Christ died for our sins.
- For believers, this restores our relationship with God because sin separates us from God.
- Because of what Jesus did we will gain eternal life.

8. Hebrews 11 deals with the subject of faith. According to the following verses, what are the three main points mentioned about faith?

Verses	Three Main Points About Faith
1	
6a	
6b	

9. With Paul back in Rome at the end of his fourth missionary journey he found himself back in a Roman prison in about A.D. 69. From there he wrote his last book which was his second book addressed to Timothy. Recall one of the purposes for writing his first letter to Timothy in Ephesus was to refute the false teachings that kept springing up. According to the following passages from 2 Timothy note the conditions Paul was facing in the Roman prison. (Continued on the next page.)

Passages	Conditions Paul faced in the Roman Prison
1:15	

4:6	
4:10	
4:14	
4:16	

Note: Conditions were severe for Christians in Rome under Nero. Some faced the lion's den as was alluded to by Paul in 2 Timothy 4:17. Many Christians were martyred, including Paul later on.

10. In 2 Timothy Paul again mentions his concerns about false teachings among the believers, persecution from Roman leaders, and pressure to conform to Roman culture. According to the following passages from 2 Timothy what action words are given to Timothy?

Passages	Actions
1:14	
3:14-17	
4:1-4	
4:5	

Note: About a year after Paul wrote his second letter to Timothy, he was found guilty of being a Christian missionary. Little is known about how Paul was executed but it occurred about 40 years after Jesus' death and resurrection. In all of the persecution Paul faced he remained true to the basic truth that salvation is obtained by the grace of God through faith in Jesus Christ. This has been the truth and foundational teaching of the Christian church from the beginning, for over 2000 years.

Session 30 Discussion Questions

1. Slavery was mentioned because it was part of Roman culture. Which of the following attributes listed below apply to people today, weather you are a student, a spouse, an employee, or whatever? We are to:
   a. Be subject to their master.
   b. Please their master.
   c. Not to back-talk to their master.
   d. Not steal from their master.
   e. Be trustworthy to their master

2. The Jewish high priests were able to forgive sins, but they were sinners too. They sacrificed "spotless" animals to gain God's forgiveness. Jesus was made perfect and was without sin. When he faced temptation he resisted. Jesus was always obedient to his Father. Therefore he was made perfect forever and was the perfect (spotless) sacrifice for all believers for all time. What else can we do to assure our sins are forgiven?

3. Faith is being sure of what we hope for even though we cannot see it. Without faith it is impossible to please God. How can we grow our faith?

4. In 1 Timothy 4-6 Paul discussed many behaviors and attitudes that are appropriate and necessary for a healthy Christian life. This letter from Paul reads like a manual for proper Christian living. What are some of the behaviors and attitudes we Christians today need to live by?

Suggested Reading for Session 31

James, 1 John, 2 John, 3 John, and Jude.

Progress:

GELNDJJR1S2S1K2K1C2CENEJPPESIJLEDHJAOJMNHZHZM-MMLJAR1C2CGEPC1T2T1T2TTPHJ1P2P1J2J3JJR

Letters from James, John and Jude – Session 31

Opening Prayer

Lord, I ask that you:
- Teach me how to follow your decrees as documented in your Word.
- Give me understanding of your Word.
- Direct me in life's paths from your Word.
- Turn my mind and heart always toward your Word.
- Keep my eyes fixed firmly on your Word.

I ask these things because I desire to keep your law, your commands, and your statutes. Help me remain faithful all the days of my life. Use my life according to your will. In Jesus's name I pray. Amen. (Psalms 119)

Introduction

In the last session we studied Paul's fourth missionary journey to Spain and then eventually back to Rome. We also reviewed his last few letters which were written to Timothy, Titus and to the Hebrews. We saw that Paul's ministry ended in Rome where he was martyred because of his faith in Jesus Christ. In this session we will review the five remaining letters found in the New Testament.

Session Material

1. Note who it was that wrote the book of James and to whom did he write it according to James 1:1?

(A) Who was the writer?_____

(B) Who was it written to?_____

_____

Note: This book was written about 20 years after Jesus' death and resurrection. Evidence points to James as being Jesus' brother.

2. James' letter, like many of the letters that Paul wrote, describes the way all Christians should live. It provides a list of practical recommendations for effective Christian living. Based on the following passages from James, note the main points that he makes. (Continued on the next page.)

Passages	James' Main Points
1:2-4	
1:5-6	
1:13-15	

1:19-20	
1:25	
1:26	
1:27	
2:14-17	
3:13-17	
4:17	
5:7-8	
5:13-16	

3. The Apostle John wrote the Gospel of John, the three letters of John, and the book of Revelation. Most likely the three letters of John were written to the churches in Asia Minor (Turkey). In 1 John the issue of false teachings is addressed. Then he reassures the believers that salvation would be obtained if they remained faithful to Jesus' teachings. Note the main point made by John in 1 John 1:8-10. _____

_____

_____

4. Read 1 John 2:15-17 and summarize the point John is making. _____

_____

_____

5. (A) In 1 John 2:18 note who it is that John is talking about. _____
   (B) Based on these passages what is he like?

Passages	What is He Like?
1 John 2:18	
1 John 2:22	
1 John 2:23	
2 John 7	

6. How do we tell if someone is an antichrist? Read 1 John 4:1-4. _____

_____

_____

7. In 2 John 1:10-11 John warns Christians about what? _____

_____

_____

8. According to 3 John 1:5-8, what complement does John give Gaius?

_____

_____

9. (A) In 3 John 1:9-10, what were John's concerns about Diotrephes?

_____

(B) List the examples given.

Examples	

10. The author of the book of Jude was probably Jude himself. He was one of Jesus' brothers as was James. According to verses 3-4 what did Jude want to write about; but what did he write about?

Want: _____

Did:_____

_____

11. Jude reminded the faithful people of three past events where God intervened to show his power and judgment on sinners. Based on the following verses from Jude, what were the examples of God's judgment on sinful people?

Verses	Examples of God's Judgment
5	
6	
7	
	Future:

12. According to the following verses from Jude, note the advice and warnings that he gives to the Christians. (Continued on the next page.)

Verses	Jude's Advice and Warnings
18	
19	

20	
21	
22-23	

Session 31 Discussion Questions

1. We are not to be enticed by the sins of the world because someday the world will be destroyed. What are some of the ways the world entices people today?

2. Some people accept God but not his son Jesus. List some examples of this antichrist attitude prevalent in our world today.

3. John was thankful Gaius was being hospitable to the missionaries. How can we also be hospitable to missionaries?

4. Jude urged the believers to remain faithful because some had allowed their faith to slip away because of godless influences. In what ways do Christians today allow their faith to slip away?

Suggested Reading for Session 32

Revelation

Progress:

GELNDJJR1S2S1K2K1C2CENEJPPESIJLEDHJAOJMNHZHZM-MMLJAR1C2CGEPC1T2T1T2TTPHJ1P2P1J2J3JJR

Revelation – Session 32

Opening Prayer

Lord God, your Word is the foundation of everything we Christians believe. Thank you for the blessing of this Bible study. As we live each day may the Holy Spirit remind us of your:

- Truths when times of trouble arrive.
- Wisdom when difficult decisions need to be made.
- Warnings about submitting to sin and temptation.
- Assurance that you always hear my prayers.
- Promise of eternal life for all of us who believe in your Son, Jesus.

Lord, may you be glorified as we grow our faith in you. May your Holy Spirit enrich the desire in us to continue to study your Word in even greater detail as we go forward. In Jesus's name we pray. Amen.

Introduction

In the last session we studied main points from the remaining letters found in the New Testament. First, we reviewed James' letter, followed by John's three letters, and finally Jude's letter. All of these letters address issues faced by the early Christian church as well as to churches today. In this session we will look into the final book of the Bible, Revelation.

Session Material

1. We started this Bible study in the book of _____ in which we saw how God created the world and everything in it. But, _____ entered into his perfect creation. God established a _____ with his people to provide a path of redemption. Later, he even sent his son, _____ to be that perfect _____ to redeem all people who believe from their sins. In the book of Revelation we see how God's plan of justice and salvation will be played out as all _____ are judged and destroyed once and for all. And, to the faithful, _____ _____ will be given as promised.

2. According to Revelation 1:1-2 who directed John to write this book?

_____

3. According to Revelation 1:3 what happens to those who read or hear the words of this prophecy and take them to heart? _____

Note: We who believe gain a sense of peace and assurance that God truly has a plan for the future and that everything is going according to his plan.

4. Based on Revelation 1:7 what is the first prophecy mentioned in this book?

_____

5. (A) According to Revelation 1:4 and 10-11 what was John instructed to do?

_____

(B) Read each of the following passages from Revelation and note if the churches were doing good or bad.

Passages	Church	Good or Bad
2:1-6	Ephesus	
2:8-11	Smyrna	
2:12-16	Pergamum	
2:18-23	Thyatira	
3:1-5	Sardis	
3:8-10	Philadelphia	
3:14-16	Laodicea	

6. In the letters to the seven churches, what promise is given to those who remain true to their faith in Jesus? See Revelation 2:7. _____

7. Revelation 4 and 5 set the stage for the rest of the book. Based on the following passages from Revelation, answer the following questions.

Passages	Questions	Answers
4:1	Where did the open door lead?	
4:2-3	Who did John first see?	
4: 4	Who sat around the throne?	
4:5	Who was positioned before the throne? (See Isaiah 11:2)	
4:6-8	Who else was positioned around the throne? (See Ezekiel 10:14 and Genesis 3:24)	
5:6-8	Who was the only one worthy to take the scroll (God's plan for the future) from God and open it?	

8. Read Revelation 6. It details some of the calamities in a symbolic manner that will be experienced by people living on earth. Now read Luke 21:8-36 which also describes events but without the symbolism. Describe conditions on earth preceding Jesus's return. _____

_____

_____

9. Revelation 8-11 continues to discuss the false teachings that will pollute the church as well as more calamities that will be experienced because of man's sin. According to Revelation 9:13-16 just how bad will conditions get? _____

_____

10. Even with the three plagues inflicted upon mankind what will be man's attitude be based on Revelation 9:18-21? _____

_____

11. According to the following verses from Revelation 13 summarize the various actions of the antichrist.

Verses	Actions of the Antichrist
12	
13	
14	
15	
16	
17	
18	

12. According to Revelation 19:11-21 who will come to put an end to the atrocities and the beasts?_____

13. According to Revelation 20:1-3 and 7-10 describe the fate of the devil and his angels. _____

_____

14. Revelation 20:11-15 describes what will happen to believers and non-believers.
(A) What is the name of the book? _____

(B) What does the book contain? _____

(C) What do the "other books" contain? _____

_____

15. According to the following verses from Revelation 21 describe God's plan to start over. (Continued on the next page.)

Verses	Details of God's Plan to Start Over
1	
2	
3	

4	
5	
22	
23	
24	
25	
27	

Note: Carefully read Revelation 22:6-12 because it reveals the purpose of this book of Revelation. The words are trustworthily and true. God sent his angel to show his servants, us, the things that must soon take place. Jesus said that he would be coming soon! Blessed are those who keep the words of this prophecy. In verse 12 Jesus said that he will give to everyone according to what he has done. May all of us continue to hunger and thirst for a greater understanding of his Word and to put his Word into action in your daily lives.

Session 32 Discussion Questions

1. The letters to the seven churches applied to the church about 2000 years ago just as it does today. How?

2. How do you know that your name is written in the "Book of Life"?

3. Now that you have completed this complete Bible study, what are some options for additional Bible study?

Suggested Reading Assignment

Start over and read the Bible daily and continue to study the Word.

Progress:

GELNDJJR1S2S1K2K1C2CENEJPPESIJLEDHJAOJMNHZHZM-MMLJAR1C2CGEPC1T2T1T2TTPHJ1P2P1J2J3JJR

This is not the end, but it is the end of your first chapter. There can be many more chapters to come as you continue to study God's Word in greater detail. All praise and glory be to you my Lord and Savior!

End Notes

Session 1--

1. beginning God created
2. alpha and omega
3. God is:

Passages	Characteristics of God
John 4:24	A spirit
1 Timothy 1:17	The King eternal, immortal, invisible, and the only God
James 1:17	Unchangeable - Immutable
Genesis 17:1 & Matthew 19:26	Almighty, all powerful - Omnipotent
John 21:17	Knows all things - Omniscient
Jeremiah 23:24	Present everywhere - Omnipresent
Leviticus 19:2	Holy
Deuteronomy 32:4	Perfect and just
2 Timothy 2:13	Faithful
Psalm 145:9	Good and compassionate
Jeremiah 3:12	Merciful
Exodus 34:6-7	Compassionate, gracious, slow to anger, abounds in love, and forgiving
Exodus 3:14	The great "I AM" who is always dependable and faithful to his followers

4. Father, Son, Holy Spirit
5. formless, void, dark...... nothing
6. (A) What was created on each day?

Day	Verses	What Was Created?
1	3-5	Light, separated day from night
2	6-8	Water and sky
3	9-13	Land and vegetation
4	14-19	Light to mark seasons, days and years
5	20-23	All water creatures and birds
6	24-31	Land animals, man and food

(B) man to be alone.
7. Man's role on this earth:

Passages	Roles and Responsibilities
Psalm 8:6-8	Rule over the earth
Genesis 1:28a	Be fruitful and fill the earth with people
Genesis 1:28b	Subdue the earth; make it a civilized place to live
Genesis 2:15	Be the earth's caretaker, steward

8.

Verses	What Does God Do for Us?
3	Watches over us.

7	Keeps us from harm.

9. God is the landlord and we are the caretakers.

10. Without faith in God it is impossible to please him. Non-believers will spend eternity in hell.

11. If we are faithful and confess our sins God will forgive us.

12. (A) God's image; (B) God wanted fellowship with man and have someone to care for his creation.

Session 1 - Discussion Questions with Thought Starters

1. Given the long list of characteristics of God, why don't all <u>Christians</u> want to get to know him better?
   - All good, healthy relationships require time. We need to make time for God through worship and prayer.
   - It is not a main priority for their life.
   - Would rather continue to live in sin.
   - Many may not understand the need for faithful obedience to God.
   - Others:

2. Given the long list of characteristics of God, why won't don't <u>all people</u> want to get to know him better?
   - All people do not know about God.
   - All people don't agree they need God.
   - They have other priorities.
   - Would rather continue to live in sin.
   - Others:

3. Have I made God a priority in my life? If not how can I do it?
   - Do I spend time in his Word every day?
   - Do I talk to God every day in prayer?
   - Is God my best friend?
   - Do I live a life that honors God?
   - Do the things I do each day bring glory God?
   - Other:

Session 2---

1. fill (populate), subdue, rule
2. tranquility and harmony.........God, nature, himself, others
3. yes

4. (A) They were not supposed to eat from the tree of the knowledge of good and evil.

    (B) obedience

5. additional details; special relationship

6. Tigris, Euphrates, Iraq

7. (A) Adam and Eve <u>were disobedient to God's command</u> to not eat from the tree of the knowledge of good and evil.

    (B) Satan

8.

Verses	God's Responses
14	He cursed the serpent, crawl on belly and eat dust.
15	He put enmity between a woman's (Mary) offspring (Jesus) and the evil one. Jesus would eventually come and destroy the evil one.
16	Pain in childbearing was greatly increased. Husbands will rule over their wives.
17	The ground was cursed and through painful toil we will grow crops for food.
18	The ground will produce thorns and thistles making it all the more difficult to produce food.
19	Hard work to produce crops only to die and return to the ground.

9.

Verses	God's Responses
8	They hid from God. They felt a sense of guilt.
10	They were afraid, fearful.
12	Blame game 1: Adam blamed Eve.
13	Blame game 2: Eve blamed the serpent.

10.

Passages	Effects
Genesis 3:23	God banished them form the Garden of Eden.
Romans 6:23a	Eternal death is the result of sin.

11. crush Satan

12. He sent his son, Jesus, to carry all of our sins to the cross and to die in place of us. Jesus said that he was the way, the truth, and the life. Only those who believe in him will ever gain eternal life with him.

Session 2 - Discussion Questions with Thought Starters

1. How do we seek independence from God like Adam and Eve?
- When we do not do God's will.
- When we ignore God's teachings.
- When we want everything done our way instead of God's way.
- Other:

2. What is God's will for my life?
- God puts desires in our hearts.
- God gives us talents and abilities to use for doing good works.

- God wants obedience.
- God wants repentance.
- God wants us to live a life that honors him.
- Learn what pleases God and do those things.
- To glorify God not ourselves.
- Other:

3. When have you ever felt separated from God?
- When not attending worship.
- When not studying his Word.
- In times of trouble and hardship.
    - Encourage students to give specific incidents.
- Other:

4. Was Adam and Eve's experience with sin any different from what we experience today?
- They experienced a period in their lives without sin.
- Disobedience to God is the same yesterday, today and tomorrow.
- Other:

Session 3--

1. Eve gave birth to two sons: Cain and Able.
2.

Verses	Major Incidences
8-9	The first murder in all of recorded history, Cain killed Able
10-12	God cursed Cain and he became a wanderer.
16	Lived in the land of Nod which was east of Eden.
17	Cain and his wife had a son named Enoch. Built a city.

3. Adam and eve had many children and Cain married one of his sisters or cousins because there were no other families on earth yet.
4. Polygamy, having more than one spouse.
5.

Time Period	Description of the Time Periods
Stone Age	A period of time before 2500 BC when man used crude tools.
Bronze Age	A period of time between 2500 BC and 1200 BC when man first started using metal tools.
Iron Age	A period of time after 1200 BC when man smelted iron to make tools and weapons.

6.

Verses	Activities
20	Lived in tents and raised livestock
21	Musicians
22	Forged tools of bronze and iron

7.

To Eve:	Lost one son but was blessed with another one.
To all believers:	From Seth's descendants came the Savior, Jesus (Mary's bloodline)

8. Methuselah, 969 years.

9.

Verses	Moral Conditions
5	Peoples' thoughts were evil.
11-12	Earth was corrupt and full of violence.

10. He was grieved, heart was filled with pain.

11. Destroy the earth with a flood but save Noah, his family, and some of every "kind" of animal and food to start the world all over again.

12. The flood.

13.

Verses	Son	Destination
2-4	Japheth	Europe and Asia
6-20	Ham	Middle East and Africa
21-31	Shem	Arabia, Asia Minor and East

14.

1. Clans	3. Nations
2. Territories	4. Languages

15.

Question	Verse	Answer
What incident is described?	9	Tower of Babel
What did the people want to do?	4	Build a tower to heaven and make a name for themselves
Why did God disapprove?	6	People showed pride and self serving behavior
What did God do?	9	God scattered the people over all the earth and caused different languages

Session 3 Discussion Questions with Thought Starters

1. Think back about your own family's ancestors and if they had lived 800 or 900 years how big would your family tree be today?
   - Very large
   - Other:

2. How far back can you trace your family tree?
   - Most families can trace back 3-4 generations.

- Other:

3. Why do we not live to be hundreds of years old like the people mentioned in Genesis?
  - God's perfect creation has deteriorated over time.
  - Sin has and still is negatively impacting the world. See Romans 8:22.
  - With so many people now on earth there is no need to live a very long time.
  - Other:

Session 4--

1. (A) Witness; (B) Link; (C) Preserve; (D) faithful and glorify
2. Shem
3. (A) A covenant is a solemn and binding agreement in which each party agrees to do certain things.
   (B) (1) nation; (2) bless; (3) name; (4) blessing; (5) bless; (6) curse; (7) blessed
   (C) Abram's responsibility: lead God's people and remain faithful to the one true God.
4.

Questions	Passages	Facts about Abram
Where was Abram from?	11:31	From: Ur (southern Iraq today) Point it out on a map.
What did God tell Abram to do?	12:1	Leave his country and go to a place God would show him.
Who went with Abram?	12:4-5a	Sarai (Sarah) his wife, Lot his nephew, and many others (relatives, servants, etc.)
To where did God lead him?	12:5b-6	Shechem in Canaan (about 30 miles north of Jerusalem). Point it out on a map.
What did God promise to give to his offspring?	12:7a	The land of Canaan
How did Abraham respond to God?	12:7b	He built an alter and worshiped God. There were no churches.

5.

Passages	Added Covenant Details
12:7	Give them the land of Canaan.
15:5	Offspring would be as countless as the stars.
17:5	Abram would be a father of many nations.
17:6	They would be very fruitful, other nations and kings would come from them
17:7	Everlasting covenant.
17:8	Canaan would be an everlasting possession; a claim Israel holds to yet to this day.
28:14a	Descendants would spread to the four corners of (all over) the earth.
28:14b	All people will be blessed through his offspring.
28:15	God will watch over them, never leave them and bring him back to the promised land.

6.

Passages	Concern and Outcome
15:2-3	Abram had no children or direct heirs.
15:4-5	God promised him countless offspring.
21:1-3	Sarai had a son and they named him Isaac.

7.

Changed from	Changed to
Abram	Abraham
Sarai	Sarah

8. (A) What: Circumcision; Why: God commanded it

(B) Purpose of this act: A sign of the covenant God made with his people. It demonstrated commitment and obedience.

Session 4 Discussion Questions with Thought Starters

1. The four T's of stewardship are: time, talents, treasures, and tithes. How do we know we are meeting God's stewardship expectations?
   - Do I have all four bases covered in my daily walk with the Lord?
   - Am I a cheerful giver?
   - Do I withhold from God?
   - God does not "need" your 4 four T's; he wants a willing and obedient heart.
   - Is it ok to substitute time for tithes?
   - Other:

2. By God's grace through faith alone are we saved according to Ephesians 2:8-10. So where do our works come into play with respect to this passage?
   - Good works are a natural by-product of our faith.
   - We want to willingly give back to God for his many blessings.
   - We want to glorify God by working to grow his kingdom.
   - Other:

3. Read James 2:17-18 and note how it explains the faith and works.
   - Faith without works is dead.
   - Can you have faith without doing any works?
   - Other:

4. Why do you think Canaan was the chosen location for the Promised Land?
   - Where Europe, Asia, and Africa converge; with many people traveling through the region making it a good place to do evangelism.
   - Other:

Session 5--

1. They would have to take possession of the Promised Land form their enemies, the Canaanites.

2. (A) They were descendants of Noah's son, Ham.

   (B) They were an immoral people who worshiped pagan gods.

3. (A) Geographically: God would give them the Promised Land.

   (B) Ethnically: They were to destroy everything; leaving no influences of pagan gods.

   (C) Religiously: They were to worship and serve the one and only true God.

   (D)The servant was to find Isaac a wife from their homeland and not from Canaan.

4.

Passages	Questions	Answers
25:21-26	What were they named?	Esau and Jacob
	Who was born first?	Esau
25:29-34	How did Jacob get the birthright away from his brother?	Esau sold it to Jacob because he wanted food.
27:1-4	What did Isaac want Esau to do and why?	He wanted Esau to prepare a special mean and then give him the family blessing (the inheritance which usually went to the first born son).
27:33-35	Who received the family blessing and why?	Jacob, because he deceived his father. He pretended to be Esau.
27:41	What was Esau's response to Jacob's deception?	He held a grudge and wanted to kill him.
27:43-45	What did Jacob do as a result?	He fled to his mother's homeland hundreds of miles away.

5. (A) Jacob was not to marry a Canaanite woman, but go to his mother's homeland and marry a cousin.

   (B) Esau married one of his step-nieces. Ishmael was his step-brother.

6.

Verses	Questions	Answers
10-12	What happened to Jacob and what did he see?	He had a dream. He saw angels ascending and descending on a stairway to heaven.
13a	Who stood at the top of the stairway?	God
13b-15	What was spoken to Jacob?	God restated the covenant he had made with Abraham and Isaac.

16-19	What was Jacob's response to this experience?	He was amazed, how awesome it must have been. He built a pillar (monument) to mark the place and called it Bethel.
20-22	What did Jacob vow to God?	He would be faithful and give a tenth of everything back to God.

7. Jacob agreed to work for his uncle for seven years for Rachel. But on the wedding night his uncle had his other daughter marry him. Jacob was required to work another seven years for Rachel.

8.

Number	Passages	Mothers	Children's Names
1	Genesis 29:32	Leah	Ruben
2	Genesis 29:33	Leah	Simeon
3	Genesis 29:34	Leah	Levi
4	Genesis 29:35	Leah	Judah
5	Genesis 30: 17-18	Leah	Issachar
6	Genesis 30:19-20	Leah	Zebulun
7	Genesis 30:21	Leah	Dinah
8	Genesis 30:4-6	Bilhah	Dan
9	Genesis 30:7-8	Bilhah	Naphtali
10	Genesis 30:9-11	Zilpah	Gad
11	Genesis 30: 12-13	Zilpah	Asher
12	Genesis 30:22	Rachel	Joseph
13	Genesis 35:18	Rachel	Benjamin

9. Israel

Session 5 Discussion Questions with Thought Starters

1. The Canaanites worshiped pagan gods. One of their rituals was to sacrifice one of their children in order to bring good luck. What god is worshiped when a baby is aborted?

- Should we put our selfish needs and wants before those of the unborn child?
- Life is a gift from God, something to be cherished.
- Fundamental reason for almost all abortions is the refusal to obey God's fifth commandment: "Thou shall not kill". Refer to Jeremiah 1:5, Psalm 139:16 and Luke 1:41-44.
- Other:

2. As part of God's covenant with Abraham, Isaac, and Jacob the Promised Land would be theirs forever. Do you think the covenant is thought to be still in effect today in the minds of many Israelite people?

- Yes, the covenant promises that the land of Canaan would always belong to God's people.
- Several Arab countries believe the land belongs to them.
- Other:

3. Question 3 above references the separation God wanted for his chosen people. Do we still need to be separated?

- Yes and no. Separated in the sense that we should not participate in ungodly or unholy thoughts and behaviors. Not separated in the sense that we need to let our light shine so that unbelievers may see our faith in action and cause in them a desire to know God for themselves.
- We need to be from this evil world but not participate in its evil ways.
- Other:

Session 6--

1. Twelve brothers and one sister.
2.

Verses	Reasons
3	His father loved him more than the others and made him a special richly ornamented robe to wear.
4	His brothers were jealous and hated Joseph.
5-8	Dream 1: Joseph would rule over his brothers.
9-11	Dream 2: Family would bow down to him making his brothers all the more jealous.

3.

Verses	Who Bought Joseph?
25-28	Ishmaelites that were in a caravan headed to Egypt.
36	Potiphar, an official of Pharaoh in Egypt.

4.

Verses	Joseph's Relationship with God
2	The Lord was with Joseph and he prospered.
3-4	Potiphar could see God was blessing Joseph so he put him in charge of everything he owned.
5	The Lord greatly blessed the Potiphar's household because of Joseph.

5.

Verses	Joseph in Prison
21	The Lord was with Joseph and he gained the favor of the warden.
22	Joseph was put in charge of the prison.
23	The Lord gave Joseph success in all that he did.

6. Joseph gives God the credit for the interpretation of dreams.
7. There would be seven years of plentiful crops followed by seven years of famine.
8. Pharaoh put Joseph in charge of the palace and all of the people in Egypt. He became the number two leader in Egypt.
9. Manasseh and Ephraim
10. The seven years of abundance was over. During the seven years of famine Egypt sold food to Egyptians and to other countries.

11.

Passages	Joseph's Reactions
43:30	Deeply moved and he wept.
45:1-3	He wept very loud.
45:14-15	He hugged and kissed them. He wept tears of joy.
46:29	He wept a long time when he saw his father, Jacob.

12.

Verses	Joseph's Insights
4-7	Joseph was sent ahead to provide a way to save his family from the famine.
8	It was God's will that Joseph ended up in Egypt and number two in command.
9-11	Joseph was in a position to provide a home for his family for the remaining five years of the famine.

13. Goshen, near the Nile River delta. Point this out on a map.
14. 70
15. Judah

Session 6 Discussion Questions with Thought Starters

1. How does God use believers and nonbelievers to accomplish his will?
- Believers:
  - Witness to nonbelievers
  - Help the needy
  - Worship and praise him
  - Set actions into motion to accomplish his plans for the future.
  - Other:

- Nonbelievers:
  - Nonbelievers crucified Jesus
  - Often used by God to awaken the faithful
  - Put in power over nations to begin their downfall
  - Set actions into motion to accomplish his plans for the future.
  - Other:

2. How do the events of Joseph's enslavement and imprisonment teach us that when bad things happen to good people they need to realize God has a plan and a purpose?
- God is in control no matter how bad it seems things seem to be.
- God can use something evil for good in our lives like he did with Joseph.
- It is hard at times for us to see God's master plan because we are involved in the tactics of the master plan's execution. It is often hard to see God's master plan.
- Other:

3. Joseph held no animosity toward his brothers. He expressed tears of joy, forgiveness, hope and love. Is this a good example for us to follow when we are wronged by someone?
- Yes, a great example, but sometimes hard to do.
- Can you think of a time when you forgave and held no animosity?
- Can you think of a time when you did not forgive and held animosity?
- Other:

Session 7--

1. (A) 430 years; (B) 70 people in all.
2.

Verses	Changes
6-7	Jacob's family grew to a large number over the centuries.
10	The Israelites were feared because they may fight with Egypt's enemies.
11-12	The Israelites were oppressed and forced into labor.
13	The Israelites were worked as slaves.
14	The lives of the Israelites were made bitter because of the hard work.
22	Pharaoh ordered all male babies of the Israelites be drowned in the Nile River.

3.

Verses	Key Events of Moses Life
1-2	He was born from the tribe of Levi (about 1526 BC). He was hidden for about three months.
3	He was set afloat in the Nile River to avoid being killed.
5-10	He was rescued by Pharaoh's daughter and was raised as her own; with his real mother caring for him.
11-14	He killed an Egyptian man for beating a Hebrew man.
15	He fled to Midian to escape Pharaoh's attempt to kill him.
21-22	He married Zipporah and they had a son named Gershom.

4.

Verses	Event Details
1-3	An angel of the Lord appeared to Moses in a burning bush.
4-9	God spoke to Moses about the suffering of his people in Egypt.
10	God wanted Moses to lead the people out of Egypt.

5.

Passages	Moses' Events	Age
Acts 7:23-24	When he killed the Egyptian.	40
Exodus 7:7	When he was called by God?	80
Deuteronomy 34:7	When he died.	120

6. Let the Israelites go free.
7.

Verses	Reasons
3	God hardened Pharaoh's heart.
5	Egyptians would see his mighty acts and know that he alone is God.

8.

Passages	Plagues
7:19	Egypt's rivers and other waters turned to blood.
8:5	Egypt overrun by frogs.
8:17	Egypt was overrun with gnats.
8:24	Egypt plagued with swarms of flies.
9:3-6	Egypt's animals died.
9:9-11	Egyptians covered in boils.
9:18	Egypt's worst hail storm ever.
10:12	Egypt covered by swarms of locusts.
10:22	Egypt cursed with three days of darkness.

9. Pharaoh would not let the Israelites go. He threatened to kill Moses.

10. All firstborn sons would die; firstborn animals too.

11. This is where Jesus instituted the sacrament of the Lord's Supper.

12. 600,000 plus women and children and many others went with them; possibly 2 million people in all. Also many farm animals.

13. (A) By day: the Lord in a pillar of cloud. (B) By night: the Lord in a pillar of fire.

Session 7 Discussion Questions with Thought Starters

1. While in Midian Moses experienced a life-changing event. He experienced God in the burning bush. Can we experience life changing events too?
- Yes when we come to know and accept Jesus as our Savior.
- An accident or death of a loved one can cause us to rethink the direction of our lives.
- We can meet another person who has a great impact on us, i.e., school teacher, pastor, future spouse, etc.
- Other:

2. God hardened Pharaoh's heart and he bitterly refused any of God's instructions. Have you ever hardened your heart toward someone or something?
- A huge disagreement with someone.
- Racism
- Prejudice
- Refuse to forgive someone.
- Other:

3. Joseph held no animosity toward his brothers. He expressed tears of joy, forgiveness, hope and love. How is this a good example for us to follow when we are wronged by someone?
- God forgives and forgets. So can I, right?
- If we refuse to forgive others, can God refuse to forgive us?
- Other:

Session 8--

1. God parted the Red Sea. The Israelites crossed on dry ground, but the Egyptian army drowned.

2.

Passages	What did God Provide?
16:13	Quail and dew.
16:14-15 & 31	Due-frost-bread; called it manna
17:6	Water

3.

Verses	Questions	Answers
8	Who was the foe?	Amalekites (Point out the region on a map. It is located in the region about 100 miles southwest of what we refer to today as the Dead Sea.)
10	Who led Israel's troops?	Joshua
13	What was the outcome?	Amalekites were defeated.

4. They established a system of judges over the people. The difficult cases were the only ones to be brought to Moses.

5.

Verses	Condition and Promises
5a	Condition: Obey God and keep his commandments.
5b	They would be God's treasured people from all people on earth.
6a	They would be a kingdom of priests.
6b	They would be a holy nation.

6. They agreed to do everything God had said.

7. The 10 Commandments.

8. They were written by God on tablets of stone.

9.

Passages	Laws and Statutes
21:2-11	Proper treatment of servants
21:12-36	Handling of personal injury disputes
22:1-15	Protection of one's personal property
22:16-31	Assuming responsibility for your actions
23:1-9	Measured justice and showing mercy
23:10-13	Laws pertaining to the Sabbath day
23:14-19	Reestablish 3 annual religious festivals

10.

Verses	Build What?	Meaning
8	Sanctuary	A holy place set apart for worship.
9	Tabernacle and furnishings	A place where God dwells among his people.

11.

Passages	What was put in or near the Ark?
Exodus 16:34	A jar of manna.
Exodus 25:16	Stone tablets of the ten commandments.
Numbers 17:10	Aaron's staff.

Session 8 Discussion Questions with Thought Starters

1. God was involved in every battle and problem his people experienced. Is God involved in our battles and problems? If so why does he allow them to happen?
- God causes the rain to fall on the good and bad.
- Bad things happen to good people.
- Test our faith.
- Build our faith.
- Allows sin to run its course. Sin has consequences.
- Other:

2. Everything in the tabernacle had a practical use as well as a symbolic meaning. What are some of the furnishings in our churches?
- Alter
- Baptismal fount
- Communion rail
- Banners
- Seasonally colored adornments
- Other:

3. God's people were to be set apart from the rest of the world. They were to be in the world but not part of what the world does. They were to lead holy lives and conduct themselves according to God's will. Does this still apply to Christians today?
- Yes, God's word remains the same for all generations.
- We live and work among nonbelievers. How can we be separate?
- We are to be in this world and let our light shine so others can see our faith in action, i.e., our good works and give glory to God.
- Other:

Session 9--

1.

Verses	Questions	Answers
1-3	Who was the leader?	Aaron
4	What did he make?	A golden calf statue, an idol to a false god.
5-6	What did the Israelites do?	Worshiped the statue.
19	How did Moses react?	Got angry and broke the tablets containing the ten commandments.
20	What happened to the calf?	Burned it, ground it to dust, and made the people drink it down with water.

26-28	What did the Levites do?	Killed 3000 of their fellow Israelites.
35	What did God do?	Inflicted a plague on the people.

2.

Verses	Questions	Answers
1a	What was Moses to do?	Chisel out two new stone tablets.
1b	What was God going to do?	Rewrite the ten commandments on the new stone tablets.
6	What is the gist of God's proclamation?	That he is compassionate, gracious, and is slow to anger.
7	Why is God the just God?	He forgives sin but sin's consequences may carry on to the third and fourth generations.
Note the three items added to the covenant:		
12	What was the first item added to the covenant?	Do not make treaties with the nations in the Promised Land.
13	What was the second item added to the covenant?	Destroy all false gods.
14	What was the third item added to the covenant?	Do not worship other gods.

3. Work six days and on the seventh day, the Sabbath, worship and honor God.

4. When the cloud, God's glory, lifted from the tabernacle it was time to move on to another destination. The cloud by day and the cloud with file by night guided the Israelites' travels.

5. Genesis; Exodus

6. Levite

7.

Passages	Offering Name	Main Purpose
1:13	Burnt Offering	Atonement for unintentional sin; and devotion to God
2:14-16	Grain Offering	Recognize God's goodness and provision.
4:13-14	Sin Offering	Forgiveness of certain sin.
5:14-16	Guilt Offering	Forgiveness of sins requiring restitution and cleansing from defilement.
7:12-13	Fellowship Offering	Act of thanks and fellowship

8. (A) Key event: Aaron was ordained into the priesthood.

(B) Why: The priests were the established link between God and man. They were to be the spiritual leaders for all religious events.

9.

Passages	Feast Name	Main Purpose
23:3 25:1-4	Sabbath	Rest for people, animals and land.
23:5-6	Passover and Unleavened Bread	Remember God's deliverance.
23:9-10	Firstfruits	Recognize God as the provider.
23:15-16	Weeks	Thanksgiving for the harvest.
23:23-25	Trumpets	Day of rest to recognize God.
23:26-27	Day of Atonement (Yom Kippur)	Cleanse people and priests, purify the Holy of Holies.

23:33	Tabernacles	Remember the journey from Egypt and give thanks for the Promised Land.
25:10-13	Year of Jubilee	Every 50th year help the poor.

Session 9 Discussion Questions with Thought Starters

1. Exodus 35:1-3 records God's command to remember the Sabbath day and keep it holy. Many Christians attend church a couple of times a month or year. Is that level of performance in keeping with God's command?
- We need to honor God with regular worship.
- Benefits of regular worship:
  - Forgiveness of sins
  - Love and honor God
  - Makes our relationship with him the highest priority because of its importance
  - Helps faith grow deep
  - Supports others in church
  - We also get support from others
- Other:

2. God punishes the guilty, even to the third and fourth generations (Exodus 34:7). Is that still the way it is today?
- The consequences of sin can span generations.
- What are some examples?
  - Father/grandfather in prison for crimes.
  - Aids
  - Unwed mother
  - Divorce
- Other:

3. Moses burned the idol, ground it to dust, and made the people drink it down with water. How are our sins eliminated?
- Through the forgiveness that only comes from Jesus.
- There is no other name under heaven by which we can be saved.
- We are not saved by works or things that we can do but by God's grace.
- Other:

Session 10--

1.

Passages	Getting organized in what ways?
Exodus 18:24-26	Developed a system of justice.
Numbers 1:2-3	Took a census for military purposes.

Numbers 1:51	Responsibilities assigned for moving the tabernacle.
Numbers 1:52-53	Encampment method around the tabernacle.
Numbers 2: 9, 16, 24, and 31	Travel in an orderly manner.
Numbers 4:4, 24, and 31	Care for the tabernacle and its contents assigned.
Numbers 8:23-26	Levite men from 25 to 50 years old chosen to work in the tabernacle.
Numbers 11:16-17	Initial political system established, 70 leaders empowered.

2. Three (Point out this next part of the journey on a map. Mount Sinai lies about 50 miles north of the southern tip of the Sinai Peninsula. They traveled north toward what we call today, Israel.)

3.

Verses	Questions	Answers
1	What was God's reaction to the complaints?	God was angry. He sent fire to consume some of the unfaithful people.
10	What did the people continue to do?	The people continued to complain.
11-15	What did Moses do?	Moses pleaded with God for help.
31-34	What did God do?	1. God provided quail meat to eat. 2. God caused a severe plague on the people because of their complaining.

4. Desert of Paran. (Point out the Desert of Paran on a map. It lied on the northwest side of what we call today the Gulf of Aqaba in east-central Sinai.)

5.

Passages	Events
13:1-2	Sent out 12 leaders (spies) to explore Canaan, the Promised Land. (They were camped in the southern edge of the Promised Land about 100 miles south of what we call today the Gaza Strip. Point this out on a map.)
13:27-29	Ten of twelve reported how fruitful the land was; that the people were powerful; and that cities were large and fortified.
13:30	Caleb wanted to go and take possession of the land.
13:31-32	But others of the twelve who had spied the land did not want to attack; they gave a bad report.
14:5-9	Joshua and Caleb encouraged the Israelites to take the land because God was with them.
14:10	The people wanted to stone Joshua and Caleb.

6.

Verses	God's Responses
20	God forgave the people.
21-24	None of that generation would ever see the Promised Land because of their disobedience toward God.
25	God told them to turn back toward the Red Sea.
29-32	Everyone 20 years and older would not enter the Promised Land except for Caleb and Joshua.
33-35	Israelites would have 40 years of wandering in the desert because of their unfaithfulness.
36-38	Ten of the twelve men who gave a false report about the Promised Land were struck down by a plague and died.

7. Moses: He struck the rock twice instead of, by faith, speaking to it for water to come out of it.

God's reaction: Moses and Aaron would not be allowed into the Promised Land.

8.

Passages	Kingdom of:	Results
20:20-21	Edom	The Israelites turned back to avoid war.
21:1-3	Arad	The Israelites destroyed the Canaanites in the Negev (point it out on a map) with God's help.
21:21-25 & 31-32	Amorites	The Israelites defeated the Amorites and settled in their lands.
21:33-35	Bashan	The Israelites defeated Bashan and took possession of their land.

9. Joshua

Session 10 Discussion Questions with Thought Starters

1. According to question number one above the Israelites spent a year learning God's laws and regulations. How long does it take a Christian to learn God's laws and commands?
   - One can learn a lot in a year.
   - It takes a lifetime to learn how to apply the Word in our lives.
   - Children need teachings from the Word beginning at a young age to instill a proper foundation.
   - Other:

2. In what ways do children suffer today because of the sins of their parents like the example found in Numbers 14:33?
   - Parents get divorced.
   - Parents ignore proper upbringing with discipline.
   - Parents fail to train their children in God's ways so that when they are older they will not depart from them.
   - Other:

3. Does it sometimes take a whole generation for a people to change like the 40 years of wandering and death in the desert?
   - Communism to democracy.
   - Culture is hard to change.
   - Sometimes 40 years is not enough time.
   - Other:

Session 11--

1. "repetition of the law"
2. Moses' request: He pleaded with God to allow him go into the Promised Land.
   God's response: God was angry with Moses and rejected his request.
3.

Verses	Instructions
5	Love the Lord with all your heart and soul.
6	Know and follow the commandments
7	Teach the commandments to your children.
8-9	Live and apply the commandments in your lives.
13	Fear (honor and respect) and serve only the Lord.
14	Do not follow other gods.
18	Do what is right and good so that it will go well with you as you take over the Promised Land.

4.

Verses	Instructions
2	Destroy them totally. Make no treaties and show no mercy.
3-4	Do not intermarry with them.
5	Destroy their idols, burn them.

5. The Canaanites worshiped many pagan gods. Total destruction of them was needed to prevent spiritual backsliding and apostasy.

6.

Verses	Reasons
6	God chose them to be a holy people to worship and serve him.
8-9	God loved them and kept his covenant with them.

7. Because God was with them every step of the way. The Arc of the Covenant was a constant reminder.

8. Cross the Jordan River and take the land,

9. (A) Be _____strong_____ and _____courageous_____.
   (B) Obey all of the __law__.
   (C) Do not __stray__ from the _____law_____.
   (D) Meditate on the __law__ day and night.
   (E) They would be prosperous and successful.

10. The people were eager, obedient, and committed to Joshua's leadership.

11.

Verses	Events
1	In Jericho the spies stayed at Rahab's house.
2-3	The king wanted Rahab to hand over the spies.
4-5	Rahab lied to the king about the spies.
6	Rahab hid the spies.
8-13	Rahab pleaded for kindness and mercy from the spies.
14	The spies agreed to protect her.
23-24	The spies reported back to Joshua that the people feared the Israelites.

12.

Passages	Blessings
Matthew 1:5	Rahab was an ancestor of Joseph, Jesus' earthly father.
Hebrews 11:31	God redeems every repentant sinner, even Rahab.
James 2:25-26	Rahab's faith was demonstrated by her deeds. Not only was she spared but also her family too.

13. God caused the Jordan River to part so the Israelites crossed it on dry ground.

Session 11 Discussion Questions with Thought Starters

1. Moses had pleaded with God to allow him to go into the Promised Land. But God refused. Is it possible for us to anger God this way too and miss out on a huge blessing because of our sins?
- Yes, sometimes we want our own will instead of following God's will.
- God has the final word about all matters.
- Sometimes our behaviors or comments are not pleasing to God.
- Other:

2. Read Deuteronomy 6:6-9. So parents, how well do you comply with this command?
- Our children need to hear and see us teaching them about God and his Son, Jesus, every day.
- Parents' actions speak louder than words.
- Sunday school is not nearly enough training.
- It is the parents' responsibility to teach them, not just the churches'.
- This is the most important learning children need to build a foundation of faith for a lifetime.
- Other:

3. God delivers on his promises with his chosen people then and still today. Our promised land is heaven. The way we eventually get there is through faith in his son, Jesus. We are still sinning today, but God has a new covenant with his people through Jesus. God is faithful and just, he forgives the sins of believers, and he grants to us eternal life. In what ways do we receive God's forgiveness?
- Pray that God will forgive us.
- Repent and turn away from sin.
- Lord's Supper
- Other:

4. What lesson does Joshua 1:7 provide to us as we live our daily lives?
- We need to be strong and courageous.
- We need to be obedient to God.

- God will make us "successful wherever you go".
- Other:

Session 12---

1.

Verses	Questions	Answers
17	Who was to be spared?	Rahab and her family. (Point out Jericho on a map.)
21	Who was not to be spared?	Every other living thing.
24a	What happened to Jericho?	Burned to the ground.
24b	What happened to precious artifacts?	They were put in the treasury of the Lord's house.

2. Ai was defeated. Everyone was killed and it was burned to the ground.
3. The Gibeonites became household servants.
4.

Verses	Outcomes
10	The Lord helped Israel defeat the southern alliance of kingdoms.
11	Many died due to a hail storm.
13-14	God stopped the sun in the middle of the day to provide more daylight hours to complete the conquest of the enemies.

5. God fought for Israel. He was helping them every step of the way.
6.

Verses	Questions	Answers
4	How large was their army?	Huge, as numerous as the sand on the sea shore.
7-8	What was the outcome?	They were totally defeated, no survivors taken.
14	What was done with the plunder and livestock?	Israelites kept it.
18	Over how many years did the battles occur?	About seven years.

7. 31
8. They were a sinful people who worshiped pagan gods.
9. The return of Jesus Christ and evil will be destroyed forever.
10. (A) No
   (B) Other surrounding lands still posed a security and spiritual threat to Israel.
11. Choose who you will serve, God or false gods. There is no in-between answer allowed with God.
12.

Verses	Successful?	Tribe
4	Yes	Judah
8	Yes	Judah (Jerusalem)
10	Yes	Judah

11-13	Yes	Othniel (First major Judge)
17	Yes	Judah
18	Yes	Judah
19	No	Judah
21	No	Benjamin
22 & 25	Yes	Joseph
27	No	Manasseh
28	No	Israelites
29	No	Ephraim
30	No	Zebulun
31-32	No	Asher
33	No	Naphtali
34	No	Dan
35	No	Joseph

Session 12 Discussion Questions with Thought Starters

1. In Joshua 24:14-15 is recorded the profound decision every living person must make: Choose for yourself right now who you will serve, God or man.
   - I choose to serve _____God_____ !

2. The first commandment warns us not to believe in other gods. What are some of the other gods that people serve today?
   - Sun and stars.
   - Created things rather than the Creator.
     - Materialism
     - Money
   - Allah who is an imaginary being.
   - The "great spirit" of the native Indians.
   - Buddha in the Hindu faith.
   - Other:

3. War is a terrible curse that we bring on ourselves. What are some of the motives for war?
   - Greed
   - Idolatry
   - Fear from Oppression
   - Ethnic cleansing
   - Power
   - Other:

4. The fifth commandment says that we are not to kill others. How is it then that God uses war as a means to an end?
- God gives life (Acts 17:25).
- God alone may take life (Job 14:5).
- God established government and empowered it to dispense justice here on earth.
  - Capital punishment (Genesis 9:6 and Matthew 26:52).
  - Just war (Romans 13:4).
- Other:

Session 13--

1. theocracy
2.

Verses	Outcomes
10	A whole generation grew up not knowing the Lord.
11-12a	The Israelites worshiped pagan gods from the people that lived around them.
12b-13	This provoked God's anger.
And the consequences were:	
14	- Israelites were defeated and plundered. - They lived in great distress, and were often ruled by pagan kings. - God was against them, allowing them to be defeated.

3.

Passages	Years of Oppression	Judge's Names	Years of Peace
3:9-11	8	Othniel	40
3:12-30	18	Ehud	80
4:1-24	20	Deborah	40
6:7-8:28	7	Gideon	40
11:1-33	18	Jephthah	6
15:1-20	40	Samson	20

4.

Passages	Samson's Events
15:14-15	He killed 1000 Philistines with a donkey's jaw bone.
16:16-17	He told Delilah about his hair.
16:21	He was captured by the Philistines, his eyes poked out, and put in chains in prison.
16:29-30	God gave him the strength to push the temple pillars down killing over 1500 Philistines and himself.

5. (A) Israel had no king like the surrounding kingdoms.
   (B) Everyone did as he saw fit.

6.

Verses	Events
1	A Levite (from Israel's priestly tribe) took a concubine.
22	Evil men (Benjamites) wanted the Levite for homosexual acts.

23-25	The Levite gave his concubine to the evil men and they raped her.
26-28	The Levite, his servant, and his concubine went home.
29-30	The Levite dismembered his concubine and sent pieces to all areas of Israel.

7.

Verses	Events
9-11	The other 11 tribes gathered together to destroy the Benjaminite town of Gibeah.
12-13	They tried to get the people of Gibeah to hand over the evil men who had committed the crimes; but they wouldn't.
After three days of battle against the Benjamites, who won?	
35	Benjamites were defeated by the army of the 11 tribes.
48	Many Benjaminite towns were destroyed

8. (A) Abducted girls from Shiloh to become their wives.
   (B) Rebuild their towns.
9. (A) She acknowledged her faith in God.
   (B) Ruth was an ancestor of Jesus' earthly father, Joseph.

Session 13 Discussion Questions with Thought Starters

1. A theocracy is a form of government when its leaders are divinely guided by a supreme religious leader. In Israel's case, God was the supreme leader. What can happen to a nation who refuses to obey God's laws and statutes?
   - Unjust laws
   - Liberal court system that eroded Christians' rights.
   - Corruption
   - Miss out on God's blessings
   - Other:

2. Why did God withhold his complete power from the Israelites and from us today?
   - God lost his patience with sinners.
   - Sin has consequences.
   - Sometimes we have to hit bottom before we decide to look up to God.
   - Other:

3. Many Israelites had departed from God's standards and rules of conduct. They became easily led astray by the influence of the pagan people still within and around the Promised Land. Can the same thing happen today?
   - Yes, the devil seeks to lead believers away from God.
   - Lukewarm Christians turn to earthly pleasures.
   - Everyone else is doing it, so why can't I?
   - Other:

4. These events from the book of Judges provide a lesson for all of mankind. Without a moral foundation to base our laws and actions, "everyone will do as they see fit". How do people do whatever they see fit today?

- Abortion: Over 40 million abortions in the Unites States.
- Divorce: About 50% of families torn apart.
- Pornography: Basis of many sex crimes to children and adults.
- Murder: The ultimate reward of greed and selfishness.
- Terrorism: Causing people to live in a constant state of fear. New laws and regulations force nude x-rays at airports.
- Homosexuality: A perversion of God's intended marriage between a man and woman.
- Greed: Casino and other forms of gambling create financial problems for many who become addicted.
- Drugs cause addictions to people and wars over the control of its trafficking.
- Other:

Session 14--

1. Gaza, Ashkelon, and Ekron. (Point out the area we call the Gaza Strip which is located near the region called Philistia.)
2. Samson
3. (1) Israelites was defeated by the Philistine army; 30,000 Israelite soldiers died.
   (2) The Arc of the Covenant was taken by the Philistine army.
4.

Passages	Positions of Leadership
3:19	Who? Samuel
3:20	Prophet – his words were respected by all.
7:9	Priest – He offered sacrifices.
7:15-17	Judge – This covered both legal and military matters.

5. 7 months
6. God helped Samuel keep the Philistines subdued for many years.
7. Who: Joel and Abijah (Samuel's sons).
   Performance: They were dishonest, took bribes, and perverted justice.
8.

Reason #	Reasons
1	Samuel was old.
2	Samuel's sons were ungodly.
3	They did not fully trust in God's leadership.

9. Samuel: Samuel was displeased.
   God: Felt rejected again.
        Ordered Samuel to grant their request for a king.
        Told Samuel to warn them about a king's power.

10. People: They still wanted a king.
    God: God told Samuel to give them a king.
11. (A) Saul
    (B)

Passages	Personal Attributes
9:1-2	He was a Benjamite; impressive without equal; and he was tall in stature.
9:15-16	He was chosen by God and would deliver the Israelites from the Philistines.
10:6	The Spirit of God changed him into a prophet. God was with him.
13:1	He was 30 years old and he reigned as king for 42 years.

12.

Passages	Saul's Actions
13:8-14	He offered a sacrifice, an act only to be performed by a Levite priest. He was impatient and would not wait for a priest.
14:24	He put his troops at an unnecessary disadvantage by not letting them eat.
15:7-11	Saul did not destroy everything as he was instructed to do.

13. (A) David
    (B) The Spirit of God departed him and an evil spirit tormented him.
    (C) Saul liked David and wanted him in his service.
14. David killed Goliath, the Philistine giant.
15. He was wounded in battle and then he fell on his own sword. His three sons
died that day too.
16. He was anointed king over Judah.
17. A long time, 7 years is the estimate.
18. 33 years over all of Israel plus 7 more years as Saul's replacement in the
south; in total 40 years as a king.

Session 14 Discussion Questions with Thought Starters

1. Joel and Abijah, Samuel's sons were dishonest, took bribes, and perverted
justice. What can Christian parents do to help our children from becoming
disobedient and evil?
   - Pray.
   - Provide a great example.
   - Manage what they read, see, hear, and do.
   - Will we always be successful? (no)
   - Other:

2. Notice in 1 Samuel 8:6-8 that God granted his peoples' request for a king. Up
to this point God was their King. Can God change his mind? Why?
   - Yes.....
   - Through repeated prayer and pleading God did allow his people to have a
     king.
   - God wants the best for his people, but sometimes we ask for the second
     best.

- Sometimes we get what isn't the best so we can learn some of life's most important lessons and mistakes.
- Other:

3. Note: 1 Samuel 8:11-17 records the burdens that were imposed on the Israelites in order to have a king. What needs to be our attitude to our government with high taxes and wasteful spending?
- Evolution not revolution, use the ballot box to cause change to happen.
- What if the government is corrupt and evil? Use legal means to help cause change to happen.
- Christians need to be a positive witness in this darkened world.
- Other:

4. Saul's life was marked with great victories for the Israelites. But, his many low points tainted his tenure as Israel's first king. How is this a good lesson for Christians today?
- Sin taints our lives too.
- We need to be steadfast in our faith till we are called home.
- We need to quickly rise up from our "tainted" actions through the forgiveness that only comes from God through his Son, Jesus.
- Other:

Session 15---

1. David and his army conquered the Jebusites in the fortress of Zion, the City of David which was later to become Jerusalem, Israel's capital city.
2. He wanted to get the Arc of the Covenant back into the City of David.
3. David's house, kingdom, and throne would endure forever.
4. King David
5.

#	Passages	Kingdoms
1	1 Samuel 30:17-18	Amalekites
2	2 Samuel 5:11-125	Philistines
3	2 Samuel 8:1	Philistines
4	2 Samuel 8:2a	Moabites
5	2 Samuel 8:5	Arameans
6	2 Samuel 8:13-14	Edomites
7	2 Samuel 12:30-31	Ammonites

6. The Lord gave David victory everywhere he went.

7. David looked to God for strength, deliverance, and wisdom. He had total trust in God.

8.

Passages	David's Failures and Consequences
3:2-5	He had six wives, and there were others too, giving new meaning to the "Family Feud".
11:1-5	He had an affair with Bathsheba who was married to Uriah, she became pregnant.
11:14-17	David put Uriah in harm's way in battle so he would be killed in action.
11:27	David married Bathsheba and they had a son.
12:7-10	The Lord sent Nathan to David to curse him: "...the sword will never depart from your house..."
12:15-18	David's first son with Bathsheba died.
12:24	David and Bathsheba had another son, he was named Solomon.
13:28-29	Absalom, David's third born son had Amnon, David's first born son, killed.
15:10-16	Absalom conspires to be king.
18:14	Absalom dies during a battle, hung in a tree.
20:1-2 & 22	Sheba's attempt to divide Israel is stopped and he was beheaded.
1 Kings 2:13-25	Solomon had his older half-brother Abonijah killed to solidify his kingship.

9. There are several ways that the Psalm 23 reflects David's faith"
- The Lord was his sheppard.
- He leads me, he restores me, and he guides me.
- I will fear no evil, for you are with me.
- You comfort.
- He was blessed even in the presence of his enemies.
- He believed goodness and mercy would always follow him.
- He believed he would spend eternity with God.

10. From David's descendants came Mary, Jesus mother.

11. Solomon

12.

#	Top Priorities
1	Make an alliance with Egypt.
2	Marry the Pharaoh's daughter.
3	Finish building the king's palace.
4	Finish building the temple of the Lord.
5	Finish building the wall around Jerusalem.

13.

Verses	God's Blessings on Solomon
12	A wise and discerning heart.
13	Riches and honor without equal among kings.
14	Long life if he remained faithful.

14.

Verses	What Solomon Did
32	He spoke 3000 proverbs and wrote 1005 songs.
33	He described life and taught about animals, reptiles, fish, and birds.
34	Many came to him to listen to his wisdom.

Session 15 Discussion Questions with Thought Starters

1. The Lord gave David victory everywhere he went. The Lord was with David in his many military conquests. The Lord is with us too when we are out fighting our daily battles. Why are we not always victorious?
   - Sin has a way of getting in the way and creating diversions.
   - God has plans for each of us. He is with us to fulfill his plans. Our behaviors may not always align with his plans.
   - David's sins created much grief for him.
   - Other:

2. The Israelite's prosperity reached a new high because David followed God and God kept his promises. If we had a truly righteous leader in our country today, would God bless us with prosperity?
   - No single person does a country make.
   - If a nation turns from its sinful ways God will heal it.
   - Just think what would happen if there was a national revival, a massive repentance and turning back to God.
   - Other:

3. A nation is truly blessed to have its leaders turn to God for wisdom and leadership. Woe to those who don't. In the United States the founding fathers realized the importance of God in the establishment of our nation. In what ways did they demonstrate their faith in God?
   - Pledge of Allegiance: "one nation under God…"
   - Money: "In God we trust".
   - Freedom of religion is a right.
   - Many Biblical quotes are inscribed on buildings and monuments across America.
   - Other:

4. Israel's twelve tribes still did not fully get along. Relations were strained. Greed and jealousy were the root causes of their disputes. If only they could have realized they had more in common than they had in differences. How does that apply to us today?
   - Greed and jealousy are tools used by the devil to drive people apart.
   - Our focus needs to be on God not on each other.
   - Much time is wasted trying to repair broken relationships.
   - Other:

Session 16--

1. (A) Proverbs; fear of the Lord; wise and the unwise
   (B) Ecclesiastes

Passages	Messages
3:1-14	There is a divinely appointed time for everything.
5:10-12 and 18-20	Greater wealth does not bring greater satisfaction. We are to be content with our blessings.
9:7-10 (Also Colossians 3:23)	Whatever you do, work at it with all of your heart as if you were working for the Lord.

   (C) Song of Songs

Passages	Examples of God's Love
John 3:16	God so loved the world that he gave his only Son to be our sacrifice for sin so that we can have everlasting life.
1 John 4:7-10	God is love, his love makes us complete.

2.

Verses	God's Main If /Then Points:
4- 5	If you remain faithful with integrity and uprightness; follow laws and decrees;
	Then I will establish your royal throne over Israel forever as promised to David.
6-7	If you or your sons turn away from me and do not observe commands and decrees, but serve other gods and worship them;
	Then I will cut off Israel from the land and reject the temple; Israel will become a byword and an object of ridicule.

3.

Verses	Solomon's Wealth
14	Much gold.
15	Revenues from merchants.
22	A fleet of trading ships.
23	Greater riches and wisdom than all other kings.
25	Many gifts of gold and other merchandise.
26	1400 chariots and 12,000 horses.
27	Silver was as common as stones in Jerusalem.

4. Polygamy, intermarriage, and idolatry.

5. Israel was divided again, ten tribes (Israel) in the northern part of the Promised Land in Canaan and two tribes to the south (Judah and Simeon).

6.

Passages	Number of Years	Kings
Acts 13:21	40	Saul
2 Samuel 5:4	40	David
1 Kings 11:42	40	Solomon
Total	120	

7. He did more evil than any of the leaders before him.

8.

Passages	Actions
16:31	He married Jezebel who worshiped Baal.

16:32	He set up an alter to Baal in the temple he built for Baal.
16:33	He made an Asherah pole and did more to provoke the Lord than anyone other king.
18:4	Jezebel killed many faithful prophets.

9. Caused a three year drought.

Session 16 Discussion Questions with Thought Starters

1. Evil has a way of reducing greatness into rubble. Many vices from Solomon's lifestyle steered him away from God. If we are not careful we too can fall away from God. What are some of the reasons that can happen to us today?
- Fail to read and study God's Word.
- Fail to attend church.
- Follow the crowd. "Everyone else is doing it".
- Fail to give back to God with our time, talents, treasures and tithes.
- Being unequally yoked with friends or spouse.
- Other:

2. Israel's prosperity gradually diminished in power and geographical influence. More importantly, Israel's faith in the one true God also diminished. Is there a correlation between faithfulness of a nation's leaders and its prominence and success?
- Faithful leaders need to rule based on God's principles.
- Lead the country based on Christian values, not based on opinion polls.
- Compromise often happens to show voters something is getting done for reelection purposes, but what is the cost later on?
- Behind the leaders are the voters. Voters are responsible to vote based on God's values not based on what seems best for me?
- Other:

3. The three-year drought was significant because the pagan god, Baal, was shown to be powerless against the one true God. Baal was considered to be the god of fertility by the pagans. The ground was not very fertile without rain. Even this was not enough to turn people's hearts back toward God. What does it take to turn hearts toward the Lord?
- The devil is a formidable foe working to steer people away from God.
- God allows sin to reign for a while, then the consequences.
- Repent and turn away from sin.
- Unless we Christians let our light shine in the presence of the lost, they may never get to know God as the true God.
- Other:

Session 17--

1.

Verses	Key Events
18-19	Elijah met at Mt Carmel with 850 false prophets.
23-24	Elijah gave the "two-bull" challenge; the real God would burn the meat (sacrifice).
25-29	Baal did not produce the fire, thus failing as a god.
30-35	Elijah soaked his alter with water three times.
36-38	God sent fire and burned the sacrifice.
39	They all fell down and confessed the real God.
40	The 850 false prophets were killed.
45	God caused the three year drought to end.

2.

Passages	Questions	Answers
1 Kings 19:19-21	Who did Elijah call into God's services?	Elisha
2 Kings 2:11-12	How did Elijah's ministry end?	He was taken up into heaven in a whirlwind. He did not experience a normal human death.
Matthew 17:1-3	What event occurred?	Elijah and Moses appeared with Jesus, the event referred to as the Transfiguration. (About 875 years after Elijah's death.)

3.

Passages	Elisha's Miracles
2:19-22	Purified the city's (Jericho's) water.
4:1-7	The woman was given an abundance of oil to pay her debts to keep her sons out of slavery.
4:32-37	Restored life to a dead son.
4:38-41	Healed a pot of stew.
5:13-14	Naaman healed of leprosy.
6:3-7	The ax head floated so that it could be found. (This was the iron age. The ax was valuable.)

4. God would maintain a "lamp" for David and his descendants forever. This refers to the covenant promise God made with David. That promise would never go dim or go out.

5.

Passages	Charges Against Israel	Consequences
Hosea 4:12-14	They were worshiping idols of pagan gods.	Daughters turned to prostitution, daughter-in-laws committed adultery. They would be ruined.
Amos 5:21-27	They offered sacrifices but were not obedient (repentant).	They would go into exile.
Micah 7:2-6	Not one godly man remained, evil abounds.	A man's enemies were members of his own household. God's judgment was coming.
Isaiah 1:1-7	The people were sinful from the soles of their feet to the top of their heads.	Country will be desolate; cities burned, and fields stripped and laid waste.

6.

Verses	Judgments
6	Samaria, the northern tribes, would be destroyed to rubble.
7	All idols, temples, and images would be destroyed.
8	Much weeping and sorrow.
9	The destruction would reach to Jerusalem, the southern tribes, too.

7.

Passages	Questions	Answers
7:10-13	What was Amos accused of by Amaziah?	That he was a prophet for hire, a false prophet, only in it for the money.
9:10	What was Israel's attitude toward these warnings from the prophets?	They ignored them. They did not believe God would allow them to be destroyed.

8. They lied, they ruled by their own authority, and the people loved it that way.

9. They were involved in stealing, murder, adultery, perjury, and worship of Baal and they thought they were safe in the temple to do all of these detestable things.

10.

Verses	Events
1-2	The Lord told Jonah to go to Nineveh a second time.
3-4	Jonah obeyed and prophesied to the people, warning them of pending disaster if they did not obey God.
5-9	The people of Nineveh repented.
10	God showed compassion and forgave the people, saving them from destruction.

11. (A) Much of the northern tribes were defeated by Assyria and many people were carried off into captivity in about 732 B.C.

(B) It was defeated by Assyria and 27,000 people were carried off into captivity in about 722 B.C.

(C) It was defeated by Babylon's King Nebuchadnezzar. Many people were carried away into captivity.

(D) Jerusalem was destroyed. The palace, temple, and all homes were burned. Many people were carried off into captivity.

Session 17 Discussion Questions with Thought Starters

1. Elijah was one of many prophets God raised up to awaken Israel out of their spiritual sleep. Does God raise-up prophets today to awaked people from their disbelief?

- Yes, "Prophet" can include ministers, evangelists, and others who teach about Jesus.
- Yes, many are called to go and spread the Good News.
- We all are to let our light shine so others can see our good works and give glory to God.
- Other:

2. Most of the 40 kings after Solomon were not faithful to God. Prophets like Elijah and Elijah tried to get Israel's kings and people spiritually back on track with their covenant with God. A number of prophets were sent by God to warn them of impending disaster if they did not change their ways. How are we to heed the same warnings today?

- God's laws apply to all generations.
- A nation whose God is the one and only true God will be blessed.
- Curses will befall evil nations. Examples:
    o The wickedness in North Korea – much hunger, no freedom.
    o Somalia's never ending wars - much hunger
    o United States – 40 million abortions – unstable economic conditions, terrorism.
- Other:

3. What were some of the consequences of sins committed today?

- Divorce and broken families.
- The negative impacts of alcohol and drug addiction.
- Pornography perverts people's minds and can lead to rape and child molestation.
- Murder takes loved ones from us.
- Other:

4. Jonah prophesied to the people of Nineveh, warning them of pending disaster if they did not turn back to God. The people of Nineveh repented. As a result God showed compassion and forgave the people. He saved them from destruction. How does this apply to people today?

- This shows how God wants all to come to faith in him and be saved.
- If we repent of our sins we will be saved.
- Repenting and believing brings us into fellowship with God.
- God will deliver a nation if it repents and turns to him.
- Other:

Session 18--

1.

Passages	Key Leaders
1:1	Adam
1:3	Noah
1:4	Ham, Shem, and Japheth

1:28	Abraham and Isaac
2:1	Jacob (Israel) and his sons
3:1	David
3:5	Solomon
8:33	Saul

2. King David's

3.

Passages	David's Key Events
11:3	He was made king over Israel.
11:4	He captured Jerusalem from the Jebusites.
14:16-17	He defeated the Philistines.
15:3	He brought the arc of the covenant to Jerusalem.
17:11-14	God promised to David that his throne will last forever through God's son, Jesus.
28:9-11	He tells his son, Solomon, to build the temple in Jerusalem.

4. It was to be of great magnificence, famous and splendor in the sight of all
nations.

5. (1) God would uproot Israel from the Promised Land.
   (2) Reject the temple.
   (3) Make the temple a byword and an object of ridicule.

6.

Verses	Questions	Answers
15	Who did God send to the Israelites to teach them?	Messengers (prophets)
16a	What was the attitude of the people toward God and the messengers?	They mocked God's messengers, despised his words, and scoffed at the prophets.
16b	As a result what was God's attitude toward the Israelites?	God's wrath was so great that there was no remedy.
17-19	What happened to the Israelites and the temple?	Many were killed and the temple was destroyed.
20-21	What happened to some of the Israelites?	A remnant of the people was taken as captives and they became servants in foreign lands for about 70 years.

7. Israel's greatness is gone. Now the people are as slaves in a foreign land.
There is much remorse and tears.

8.

Verses	God's Judgments
2	God showed no piety in his wrath.
3	In God's fierce anger he cut off Israel.
4	God treated them like an enemy or foe.
17	God did what he planned to do if the people were unfaithful. He showed no pity.

9. God would not forgive the Israelites. Their prayers were not getting through to
God.

10. Israel's punishment would end.

11.

Passages	Words of Hope
Isaiah 1:25-27	Jerusalem would be restored and the people redeemed.
Jeremiah 24:1-7	God would restore a remnant of his people in the Promised Land.
Ezekiel 43:6-9	God promised to live among the Israelites forever.

12. 70 years; 70 years

Session 18 Discussion Questions with Thought Starters

1. God's people mocked God's messengers, despised their words, and scoffed at the prophets. As a result God's wrath was so great that there was no remedy for their sins. How does the same thing happen today?
- When preaching and teaching from the Word is ignored.
- When people are lukewarm in their faith.
- Only one unforgivable sin, rejecting God.
- Faith without works is dead.
- Other:

2. Because of his anger, God cut off his people. He treated them like an enemy. He did what he planned to do if the people were unfaithful. He showed no pity. We too will be destroyed if we do not remain faithful. What can happen?
- Life can be made more difficult because of the poor choices we make.
  - Gay marriage
  - Abortion
  - Drug addiction
  - Stealing
  - Murder
  - Etc.
- Sin has negative consequences.
- The unfaithful will be sent to hell, eternal separation from God.
- Other:

3. The Israelites prayers did not get through to God because of his anger toward them. They had gone too far into sin and God refused to listen to them. In what ways can we demonstrate our faithfulness to God based on the following four categories?
- Time - for prayer, Bible study, worship, showing kindness, etc.
- Talents - helping others, teaching, witnessing, etc.
- Tithes & Treasurers – giving back to God, helping others who are need, etc.
- Testimony- in words and deeds, pray with others, share your faith with others, etc.

Session 19--

1. Cyrus, King of Persia
2. Teacher, priest, and expert in the Law of Moses
3.

Passages	Questions	Answers
Ezra 2:64	About how many people were in the first group to go back to Jerusalem?	About 50,000
Ezra 1:3	What was their top priority?	Rebuild the Temple
Ezra 3:8	Who was their leader?	Zerubbabel
Matthew 1:12 (Luke 3:27)	What was significant about him?	He was part of Jesus' ancestry.

4. (A)

Passages	Key Events
Isaiah 44:26-28 and 45:1 & 13	Isaiah prophesied about 200 years earlier that a man named Cyrus would restore Jerusalem.
Daniel 3	Shadrach, Meshach, and Abednego survived the fiery furnace and King Nebuchadnezzar acknowledged God's power.
Daniel 5	Daniel interpreted the king's dream; that the Medes and Persians would defeat Babylonia.
Daniel 6	Daniel survived the lions' den and King Darius issued a decree that all people must fear and revere the living God, Daniel's God.
Ezra 1:2	God told him to build a temple in Jerusalem.

(B) King Cyrus remembered the key events above and received directions from God. This was all the encouragement he needed to do the right thing. He respected the God who controls all of life's events.

5. Those returning from the exile did not remain faithful. They intermarried with nonbelievers.

6. They sent the non-believing women and children away.

7. (A) Governor

(B) He rebuilt the walls and gates of the city.

8.

Passages	Thankful Actions
8:18	Ezra read the Book of the Law to the people for seven days.
9:1	They fasted.
9:2	They confessed their sins and wickedness to God.
9:3	They read from the Book of the Law for a quarter of the day and worshiped God for a quarter of the day.
10:29	They made an oath to follow the Law of God, obey the commands, regulations, and decrees of the Lord.
10:37	The people promised to tithe their increases.

9.

Passages	Questions	Answers
1:19	Who was king of Persia?	Xerxes
2:5-7	Who raised Esther?	Mordecai who was a Jewish cousin.

2:10	What was Esther's nationality?	Jew
2:17	Who became queen of Persia?	Ester
3:8-10	What did Haman want to do?	Destroy the Jews.
7:1-4	What did Esther do?	She asked the king to stop the plan to kill the Jews.
8:7-11	What was the result?	- Haman was hanged. -The king gave the Jews freedom, even to have their own army.

10. 127 provinces stretching from India to Cush (Ethiopia), including the Promised Land. (It was about the size of the 48 states in the United States.)

11. Authorship to some of the books has been debated, but the most likely authors are shown here except for the book of Job.

Book Name	Author
Job	Unknown
Psalms	David mostly.
Proverbs	Solomon
Ecclesiastes	Solomon
Song of Songs	Solomon

Session 19 Discussion Questions with Thought Starters

1. In this session we saw how God arranged international events that would enable the remnant of the Israelites to return to their homeland. In what ways does God orchestrate international events today?

- God chooses kings and rulers.
- God allows nations to drift away from him.
- God wants all nations to come to him and believe in him.
- God can heal lands if the people will repent.
- Other:

2. King Cyrus remembered the following key events:
   a. Shadrach, Meshach, and Abednego survived the fiery furnace.
   b. Daniel interpreted the king's dream; that the Medes and Persians would defeat Babylonia.
   c. Daniel survived the lions' den.

And, after receiving directions from God he let Israelites go back to their homeland. He respected the God who controls all of life's events. What is the colossal message in those events that we would be well to remember?

- We can read about all God has done for his people and be assured he is there for us today.
- We can make plans but it is God who directs us each step of the way.
- God will never leave us or forsake us who are his faithful followers.

- We may experience trials and tribulations too because God has a purpose for them.
- All things work out for the good to them who love the Lord.
- Other:

3. Those returning from the exile did not remain faithful. They intermarried with nonbelievers. God was concerned that non-believing spouses would lead them away from faith in God. Does this apply today? If yes, how?
- Marriage at times is hard enough without adding in differences of religion.
- We really need to be "equally yoked" with our spouses.
- There always is the risk that the nonbeliever will draw the believing spouse away from God.
- Other:

Session 20--

1.

Verses	Questions	Answers
1	Was Job a God-fearing man?	Yes
2	How many children did he have?	7 sons and 3 daughters.
3	How wealthy was Job?	Enormous wealth, livestock, and many servants.

2.

Verses	Events faced by Job
13-15	Ox and donkeys stolen and servants killed.
16	Sheep and servants burned up.
17	Camels stolen and other servants killed.
18-19	Sons and daughters died due to a storm.

3. He was full of sorrow and grief. He praised God and did not blame him.

4. (A) Job got sores all over his body.
   (B) His wife told him to curse God and die.
   (C) Job remained faithful to God.

5. Remain joyful, pray for relief and give thanks to God for it is his will for you in Christ Jesus.

6.

Passages	Lessons
5:17	Blessed are those who are disciplined by God. Discipline helps us grow in our faith.
19:25-27	We can be confident that in the end, we will be saved. We will spend eternity with God.

7.

Verses	Job's Blessings
10	God gave him two times more than he previously had.

11	His family comforted and consoled him. He was given silver and gold.
12	He had thousands of sheep, camels, oxen, and donkeys.
13	He had seven new sons and three new daughters.
16	God granted him a long life, 140 years; and he saw many of his descendants.

8.

Verses	Questions	Answers
20	What was to happen to false prophets?	They were to be put to death.
21-22	How are we to know if a prophet is from God?	If the prophecy does not happen then he is not from God. God's prophets are 100% accurate.

9. (1) Point them out on a map.

Passages	Nations
1:5	Aram
1:8	Philistines
1:9-10	Tyre in Phoenicia
1:11	Edom
1:13-15	Ammon
2:1-2	Moab

(2) Habakkuk's complaint: How long would God allow Israel's evil and wickedness to prevail?

God's response: The Babylonians would conquer Israel.

(3) God would restore Judah and never again would his chosen people be shamed.

(4) He foretold the birth of Jesus.

(5) The dead will be resurrected and only believers will inherit everlasting life with Jesus. All unbelievers will be doomed to eternal damnation.

10. (A) John wrote Revelation

(B) Jesus spoke the prophecy in Matthew 24.

Session 20 Discussion Questions with Thought Starters

1. Job had it all. But, God allowed his faith to be tested in some very difficult ways. How does God tenderize our faith today?
- May lose a loved one to death.
- May suffer form an illness.
- May lose wealth or possessions.
- May lose a job.
- Other:

2. How can suffering and troubles make us a stronger Christian?
- God allows troubles and suffering to occur to his faithful followers to:
  (1) Punish us because of our sins;
  (2) Test our faith as he did in Job's case;
  (3) To discipline us to grow our faith.

- Positive as well as negative experiences help us grow in wisdom.
- Experience is sometimes the best teacher.
- Other:

3. When Job lost almost everything he was full of sorrow and grief. But he praised God and did not blame him. He praised the name of the Lord. Is this attitude applicable to us today?
- Yes, God disciplines those he loves.
- All things will work out for the good, according to God's plans.
- We can be confident that in the end, we will be saved.
- God is in control.
- Other:

4. When we listen to evangelists who prophecy today, how are we to know if a prophet is from God?
- Everything he says must come to pass.
- 100% accuracy of their predictions is the standard for a prophet from God.
- Is what is being preached correctly interpreted form God's Word?
- Someone who predicts the day the world will end contradicts what the Bible says; that only God knows when the end will occur.
- Other:

Session 21--

1.

Dates B.C.	People	Notes
4000	Adam and Eve	They were the first created humans in God's image.
3000	Noah	He and his family survived the flood.
2166-1991	Abraham	Covenant established with God. First son was Ishmael.
2066-1886	Isaac	Almost sacrificed by Abraham.
2006-1856	Jacob	Father of the 12 Tribes, his name was changed to Israel.
1915-1805	Joseph	He was a slave but he rose to become the number two leader of all of Egypt.
1876-1446	Israelites	In Egypt 450 years, became slaves.
1526-1406	Moses	God used him to facilitate the ten plagues on Egypt and lead the journey to the Promised Land.
1375-1050	15 Judges	Samuel was the last judge.
1050-1010	King Saul	Israel's first king started strong but had a weak finish.
1010-970	King David	He was promised an everlasting throne by God. He defeated all of the surrounding pagan nations.
970-930	King Solomon	He was king during Israel's peak of prosperity as a nation.

930-586	20 Northern Kings-Israel and 20 Southern Kings-Judah	After Solomon's reign, Israel split in two. In 722 Assyria conquered Northern Kingdom. In 612 Babylon conquered Assyria. In 586 Jerusalem (Southern Kingdom) is conquered by Babylon.
16 Prophets		
539	Israelites	Persia conquered Babylon.
538	Zerubbel	Group 1 returned to Jerusalem.
516	Israelites	Temple was rebuilt.
473	Esther	Jews saved from massacre by the Queen.
458	Ezra	Group 2 returns to Jerusalem.
432	Nehemiah	Group 3 returns to Jerusalem.
539-330	----------	Persian period of rule.
330-167	----------	Greek period of rule and Hellenism spreads.
167-63	----------	Maccabean period.
63 B.C. & onward	----------	Roman period.

Dates	People	Notes
B.C. 5	Jesus	The approximate date the Savior was born.
A.D. 26	Jesus	The approximate date he was baptized.
A.D. 28	Jesus	The approximate date he was crucified.
A.D. 35	Paul	He was a Jew but he converted to Christianity
A.D. 95	John	He wrote the book of Revelation.

2.

Passages	Prophecies
Genesis 3:14-15	God would send his son, Jesus, to destroy the devil's work.
Numbers 24:17-19	The star that would come out of Jacob will be Israel's deliverer, that being Jesus.
Deuteronomy 18:15	God was to rise up a prophet that must be listened to, that being Jesus.
2 Samuel 7:16	God promised to David that his throne would last forever, through his descendant, Jesus.
1 Kings 9:5	God promised to Solomon that his throne would last forever, through his descendant, Jesus.
Psalm 2	Foretells of the coming Son of God, Jesus, and the power he will have.
Psalm 16:9-11	Reference is made to Jesus' resurrection.
Psalm 22:1, 16, 18	Depictions of events during Jesus' crucifixion.
Psalm 89:3-4, 27-29	David's throne will endure forever through God's first born, Jesus.
Isaiah 7:14	Depicts the virgin birth of God's Son, Jesus.
Isaiah 9:6-7	Foretells the birth of the child, Jesus, who will reign on King David's throne forever.
Jeremiah 23:5-6	Foretells the birth of Jesus, a king from the line of David and he will be called: The Lord our Righteousness.
Ezekiel 37:24-28	A descendant of David will be king and their God, and they will live in the Promised Land forever.

| Micah 5:2-5 | Out of Judah will come the ruler over Israel and he, Jesus, will be their shepherd in the strength and majesty of the Lord. |
| Zechariah 9:9 | Foretells of the triumphal entry of their king, Jesus, into Jerusalem. |

3. No, most of the people were looking for a king like King David who would defeat the Romans and reestablish the nation of Israel like it was in former days. God had a better plan for his Son, Jesus, to establish a kingdom that will last forever.

Session 21 Discussion Questions with Thought Starters

1. Why is it a good idea to study the Old Testament books of the prophets?
- To see the unity in the prophecies of so many different men who lived at different times and in different places.
- They build up our faith in God's Word, showing that God keeps his promises.
- God's Word is always edifying to our overall understanding of his plan of salvation for those who believe.
- Other:

2. So many times did the Israelites wander from God's laws and statutes. The consequence of it all was a crushed nation. It would never to be the same. How can a pagan nation today regain its prosperity?
- Read 2 Chronicles 7:14-15.
  - God promises to forgive their sins.
  - God promises to heal their land.
  - God will listen to their prayers.
- People need to realize that God is really in control.
- Can a nation lose its prosperity?
  - Yes, if it turns away from God.
- Other:

3. Kingdoms come and they go. Egypt, Israel, Babylon, Assyria, Persia, Greece, Rome and many others over recorded history have lost their standing as the most powerful nation in the world. How can the United States lose its position as the world leader?
- Like Israel, by wandering away from God's laws and statutes.
- By not embracing the true God who wants his church evangelizing the world.
- Failure to repent of sin.
- Other:

Session 22---

1. Matthew, Mark, Luke, and John
2. God sent his Son to save the lost.
3. (A) Joseph's
   (B) Adam and Eve
4.

Verses	Questions	Answers
26	Who visited Mary?	The angel, Gabriel.
31	What was Mary told?	She was to have a son, and he was to be named Jesus.
35	What was Mary told?	The Holy Spirit would create the pregnancy. Without any sin the child would be called the Son of God.
38	What was Mary's response?	She willingly accepted her assignment as would a faithful servant.

5.

Verses	Questions	Answers
19	After hearing of Mary's pregnancy, what was Joseph inclined to do?	Divorce Mary.
20-21	Who convinced him to do otherwise?	An angel of the Lord.
22-23	Which prophet foretold this event?	Isaiah about 700 years earlier. (Isaiah 7:14 and 8:8)
24-25	What was Joseph's response?	He was obedient and married Mary.

6.

Verses	Questions	Answers
4	What town was Jesus born in?	Bethlehem, a small town about 5 miles south of Jerusalem.
7	Why was Jesus laid into a manger?	There was no room for them at the inn.
8-16	Who first came to see Jesus?	Shepherd's; symbolic of Jesus' future role as the shepherd of his flock of all believers.
17-18 & 20	What was their response?	They spread the news, and the people were amazed. They praised and glorified God.
19	What was Mary's response?	Mary treasured these things and pondered them in her heart.
21	On Jesus' eighth day what happened?	He was named "Jesus" and circumcised.
22-24	On Jesus' 40th day what happened?	According to the law he was consecrated to the Lord and a sacrifice was offered for Mary's purification.

7.

Verses	Questions	Answers
1-2	Who came from the East to see Jesus?	Magi from the east.
3-4	Why was King Herod and "all" Jerusalem disturbed?	They felt threatened that a new king was born.
5-6	Which prophet foretold Jesus' birth in Bethlehem?	Micah (Micah 5:2)
11	When the visitors came to see Mary and Jesus, where were they staying?	This occurred some months after Jesus' birth. They were staying in a house.
11-12	What three things did the visitors do?	1. Bowed down and worshiped him. 2. Presented gifts of gold frankincense, and myrrh. 3. Returned to their country by a route that avoided King Herod.

Session 22 Discussion Questions with Thought Starters

1. Mary willingly accepted her assignment and went on to be a faithful servant.
How does she provide an excellent role model for us?
- She obeyed God without question.
- She demonstrated her faith in this great act of obedience.
- She followed through to completion. She suffered only as a mother can at the foot of her Son's cross.
- Other:

2. There was no room for Joseph and Mary at the inn. If they only knew who it was that they turned away. How can we make room for Jesus in our lives?
- Regular worship, at least weekly.
- Pray without ceasing in Jesus' name.
- Let our light shine by doing good deeds to those in need.
- Regular study of God's word.
- Other:

3. The shepherds spread the news, and the people were amazed. They also praised and glorified God. How can we spread the good news and glorify God?
- Take advantage of situations that we are confronted with to tell people of God's saving grace through Jesus.
- We need to know what pleases God, then follow through and do acts of mercy.
- We need to support the training of pastors, evangelists, and missionaries.
- Other:

Session 23---

1.

Verses	Questions	Answers
13-14	Who warned Joseph to escape to Egypt?	Angel
15	Who was the prophet referenced in this verse?	Hosea 11:1
16	What evil action did King Herod order?	He had all boys up to two years old killed in and around Bethlehem.
17-18	Which prophet foretold this event?	Jeremiah 31:15
19-23	After the king died where did the angel tell Joseph take his family to live?	Nazareth (Reference Isaiah 53:3 and Psalm 22:6. Nazarenes were despised.)

2.

Verses	Questions	Answers
49-50	At 12 years old what profound announcement does Jesus make to his parents?	Jesus declares his relationship to his Heavenly Father.
48 & 50	What was Jesus' parent's reaction to what he was doing and what he said?	They were astonished and they did not understand what he was saying.
51	What personality characteristic of Jesus is mentioned?	Obedience
52	In what other ways did Jesus grow up?	He grew in wisdom and stature; and in favor with God and men.

3.
(A) Jesus' hometown was _____Nazareth_____.
(B) Jesus' dad was a _carpenter_____.
(C) Jesus had _____4_____ brothers.
(D) Jesus had _some_ sisters.

4.

Verses	Questions	Answers
11-15	What was promised to Zechariah and Elizabeth?	They would have a son, to be named John (later known as John the Baptist, Jesus' cousin).
19	Who told Zechariah about this?	Gabriel the angel.
16-17	What was John's mission to be?	- Lead many people back to the faith. - Prepare the people for the coming of the Lord.

5.

Verses	Key Points
20	Because his strong preaching and teaching they wondered if he was the Christ. He made it clear that he was not the Christ.
23	His job was to prepare the way for the Christ.

6.

Verses	Questions	Answers
21	Who did John baptize?	Jesus
22	Whose voice did they hear?	God's voice, declaring Jesus as his Son.
23	How old was Jesus when this occurred?	About 30

7.

Verses	Temptation	Bible References	Jesus' Responses
1-4	Food	Deuteronomy 8:3	God would provide for his needs.
5-7	Jump off the temple roof without injury.	Deuteronomy 6:16	We are not to test (tempt) God.
8-10	All of the kingdoms of the world.	Deuteronomy 6:13-15	Worship only God.

8.

Passages	Jesus's Ministry
2 Corinthians 8:9	He was poor.
Luke 4:28-30	They attempted to throw him off a cliff, to kill him.
Isaiah 53:3	He was despised and rejected.
John 8:58-59	They attempted to stone him to death.
Matthew 8:20	He had no home.
Matthew:13 1-2	He drew large crowds.
Matthew 13:57	He was not respected in his home town.

Session 23 Discussion Questions with Thought Starters

1. At 12 years old Jesus wanted to be in the temple but his parents wanted him to go home with them. They did not fully understand who their son was. But God, with all things under his control, wanted his Son to obey his parents. How do we demonstrate our obedience to God in our daily walk with him?
- Keep the commandments.
- Daily prayer.
- Daily acts of charity and kindness.
- Do all to God's glory, not our own.
- Worship regularly.
- Other:

2. Jesus grew in wisdom, stature and in favor with God. In what ways can we continue to grow regardless of our age?
- Study his Word daily in our lives.
- Applying God's principles to our lives.
- Gain the experience of helping others.
- Pray that God will bless us with wisdom and knowledge.
- Other:

3. Jesus met and defeated temptation with the truth found in God's Word. What truths from the Word help us resist temptation?
- When tempted God provides a way out. (1 Corinthians 10:13)
- Pray for God to put a hedge of protection around you. (Hebrews 2:18)

- Be aware of temptations. Know your weaknesses. (Galatians 6:1)
- Watch and pray so you will not fall into temptation. (Matthew 26:41)
- Do not love the "world". (1 John 2:15-17)
- Other:

Session 24--

1. (A) He began forming his group of disciples.
   (B) Disciple
2. (A) 72
   (B) Jesus designated 12 disciples as apostles.
   (C) Apostle
3. How: Jesus gave them power and authority to drive out demons and cure diseases.
   Why: Jesus sent the Twelve out to preach from village to village.
4. No, some were not ready to fully accept Jesus' teachings.
5. Very successful, even demons submitted to the disciples.
6. Jesus cleared out the merchants and money changers from the temple.

7.

Passages	Jesus's Preaching
Matthew 4:23-25	Large crowds followed him.
Matthew 5:1 thru 7:29	The crowds were amazed because he taught as one who had authority, not like other teachers.
Matthew 9:35-36	Crowds sought Jesus. He was teaching, preaching, and healing many. He had compassion on them because they were harassed and helpless.

8. Parables
9.

Passages	Principles
Mark 4:2-8 & 14-20	The parable of the sower refers to the different ways people will receive the gospel. Some will hear and remain faithful. Some will hear and fall away.
Luke 15:11-32	The parable of the lost son illustrates the patience the father (God) has for his errant children. God is always ready to receive us back if we drift away from him.
Matthew 20:1-16	The parable of the workers in the vineyard illustrates the message of the landlord's (God's) generosity to those who come to faith early or late in life.

10.

Passages	Incidents	Outcomes
John 4:4-42	Jesus talked to the woman at Jacob's well.	Many people came to faith because of the woman's testimony.
Luke 7:36-50	The sinful woman washes Jesus' feet.	Her sins were forgiven and her faith in Jesus saved her.

John 12:1-8	Jesus's friends give him a dinner in his honor and Mary put perfume on Jesus's feet.	Jesus reveals his pending death to his friends.
Mark 10:13-16	Jesus corrects the disciples about children.	Jesus put his arms around the children and blessed them.
John 11:32-44	Jesus cries for his friends.	Many people witnessed God's glory when Lazarus was raised from the dead and many came to believe in Jesus.

Session 24 Discussion Questions with Thought Starters

1. Jesus demonstrated courage when he stood up for his convictions as he drove the merchants and money changers out of the temple. How can we demonstrate our courage of our convictions?
- Practice what pastor preaches every day.
- Vote for Christian leaders who will follow God's laws and statutes.
- Respectfully speak up and be willing to be a positive witness of God's truth in discussions with family, friends, and others.
- Let our light shine by our good works so that God will be glorified.
- Other:

2. Based on John 6:53-71 not all of Jesus' disciples remain faithful. Some fell away. Apparently they were not ready to do what it takes to be a follower of Jesus. What does it take to be a follower of Jesus?
- Faith that Jesus died and rose again to save the lost, of which I was one.
  - We have nothing to lose and everything to gain with faith in Jesus.
- Faith that Jesus is awaiting our arrival to heaven to usher us into everlasting life.
- Faith that Jesus is our only mediator between God and us. He intercedes for us when we pray.
- Faith that Jesus will be there when we are happy and when we are hurting. He is our best friend.
- Other:

3. The parable of the lost son illustrates the patience the father (God) has for his errant children. God is always ready to receive believers back if they drift away from him. Is there any unforgivable sin?
- Yes, only one and it is the rejection of God.
- God allows people to go down a path of sin for a while. At some point these people demonstrate by their behavior that they would rather have their sinful lifestyle than lead a righteous life.
- Other:

Session 25--

1.

Passages	Who	What
Matthew 9:27-31	Two men	Blindness
Mark 2:3-12	Man	Paralytic (let down through the roof)
Luke 13:11-13	Woman	Crippled for 18 years
John 4:47-53	Official's son	Sick, close to death

2.

Passages	Who	What
Matthew 17:14-18	Son	Seizures, demon possession
Mark 5:1-15	Man who lived in the tombs	Demon possession, a legion of demons
Luke 4:33-37	Man in the synagogue	An evil spirit

3.

Matthew 8:23-27	He calmed the storm.
Mark 6:47-51	He walked on water and the wind died down.
Luke 9:12-17	He fed 5000 people with enough food for 5 people.
John 2:1-11	He turned water into wine.

4.

Passages	Who
Mark 5:22-24 & 38-42	Jairus' 12 year old daughter
Luke 7:11-15	Widow's son
John 11:1-44	Lazarus

5. So many that the whole world could not hold them all.

6. Build our faith in Jesus, the Son of God. With that faith we are guaranteed a place with him for all eternity in heaven.

7.

Passages	Day	Events
John 12:12-17	Sunday	Jesus entered Jerusalem on a colt (Palm Sunday).
Mark 11:15-18	Monday	Jesus cleared out the merchants and money changers from the temple.
Matthew 21:23-27	Tuesday	Jesus authority is questioned by the chief priests and elders.
Luke 22:1-6	Wednesday	Judas plots against Jesus.
Mark 14:12-25 & 43-46	Thursday	- The Lord's Supper in the upper room. - Jesus was arrested.
Matthew 27:27-66	Friday	Jesus's crucifixion, death, and burial (Good Friday).
Luke 24:1-12	Sunday	Jesus's resurrection, the tomb was found empty (Easter Sunday).

8.

Passages	When	Who
John 20:10-18	Sunday	Mary Magdalene
Luke 24:13-35	Sunday	Cleopas and another man
Luke 24:36-43	Sunday	10 Disciples
John 20:26-29	Week Later	11 Disciples (including Thomas)

John 21:1-24	Later	Some Disciples
Matthew 28:16-20	Later	11 Disciples
1 Corinthians 15:6	Later	Over 500 brothers
1 Corinthians 15:7	Later	The Apostles, James, and Paul
Acts 1:3-11 & Luke 23:50-52	40 days after resurrection – Jesus' ascension to heaven	The Apostles

9. Jesus died to atone (make amends) for the sins of all believers. Sin separates us from God so he sent his only Son to die in our place. Whoever believes in Jesus will not die but will gain everlasting life. (John 3:16)

10. In heaven, seated on God's right side.

Session 25 Discussion Questions with Thought Starters

1. Even though everything Jesus did during his ministry was not recorded, enough has been written to capture the divine acts of love and sacrifice to show all people for all time the plan of salvation he provided. The Bible documents all we need to know to gain his blessed assurance of forgiveness and everlasting life. What position do we need to take when someone mentions another book as having the truth about our faith?
- Only God's Word, the Bible is the truth.
- Other books may hold some truths but not all truth.
- Examples of other books: Koran and Book of Mormon
- Other:

2. How does someone who does not yet believe get saved?
- Someone needs to witness to them about Jesus.
  - See the last "Note" in this session....above.
- They need to hear the spoken word of God.
- Begin a relationship with Jesus by reading the Bible.
- Prayer from family, friends, or others that God would set up circumstances that will help them be receptive to the Gospel.
- Pray that the Holy Spirit would help them.
- Repent of their sins and begin leading a life worthy of God's forgiveness.
- Other:

3. If you get engaged in a conversation about Jesus with an unsaved person, some of the discussion you have with them in noted above. How should you follow-up with the new Christian?
- Talk with them often but don't be a pest.
- Gently offer ways that they can grow spiritually.
  - Attend church with you.
  - Attend Bible study with you.
  - Attend Christian gatherings with you.
  - Introduce them to other Christians.

o   Listen to them about their troubles and fears.
o   Council them as you are led by God.
o   Other:

Session 26--

1. Make disciples in all nations, baptize them, and teach them.
2. Jesus was building his church and it would last forever.
3.

Passages	Who is the Rock
Colossians 1:15-18	Christ is head of the church.
Deuteronomy 32:3-4	Lord our God
2 Samuel 22:2-3	Lord
Psalm 19:14	Lord my Redeemer
Psalm 92:14	Lord
Isaiah 26:4	Lord

4. We are to use our gifts, talents and abilities, to help the church "go and make disciples" all over the world.
5. Luke, 30 years.
6. The disciples were still looking to Jesus to restore the Israelite kingdom back to what it was like during King Solomon's reign. Jesus planned to build a spiritual kingdom, his church.
7.

Verses	The Early Church
42	Many people were devoted to the teachings and fellowship.
43	Miracles were done by the Apostles.
44	They had harmony and unity.
45	They gave to the needy.
46	Met daily, shared meals, and were glad and sincere.
47	They praised God and enjoyed each other; their numbers grew daily.

8. They were highly regarded, many became believers, and many were healed. God blessed their evangelistic efforts.
9.

Passages	Persecution
Acts 5:17-20	Apostles were put into jail.
Acts 7:54-60	Steven was stoned to death.
Acts 8:1	Persecution was great, most of them scattered, some went underground
Acts 8:3	Saul (Paul) started to destroy the church by putting believers into jail.
Acts 9:1-2	Saul threatened to murder the disciples.

10. James and John
11. He preached to the people. He quoted the prophets, preached the Gospel, and urged them to repent and be baptized.
12. Peter was bold and courageous as he spoke the truth about Jesus.

13.

Passages	Advice
1:14-15	Be holy.
2:1-3	Grow your faith.
2:13-15	Submit to the legal authorities.
3:1	Wives are to be submissive to their husbands.
3:7	Husbands are to be considerate and respectful to their wives.
3:8	Live in harmony with each other in love; be sympathetic, compassionate and humble.

14. (A)

Verses	Peter's Instructions
13	Be eager to do good works.
14	Do not be frightened, if you suffer for doing what is right you will be blessed.
15	Be prepared to tell others why you have hope. Do it with gentleness and respect.
16	Keep a clear conscience by doing what is right.

(B) We do these things because we will be overjoyed and blessed when we are saved from eternal punishment.

Session 26 Discussion Questions with Thought Starters

1. Peter was bold and courageous as he spoke the truth about Jesus. How is that an example for us to follow today?
- We should not be afraid or ashamed of the Gospel.
- We need to be sensitive to opportunities to share our faith.
- Share your faith with a tender, sensitive approach; not with a club.
- We need to stand firm and not compromise God's truth.
- Other:

2. What advice should we give our fellow Christian friends and family about how to live according to their faith?
- Be holy.
- Worship regularly.
- Study God's Word.
- Continue to grow your faith.
- Submit to the legal authorities.
- Wives are to be submissive to their husbands.
- Husbands are to be considerate and respectful to their wives.
- Live in harmony with each other in a spirit of love.
- Be sympathetic, compassionate and humble toward each other.
- Other:

3. If we are ever faced with persecution for our faith, what good advice can you give to help survive through it?

- Love your enemies.
- Do good to those who hurt you.
- Be eager to do good works.
- Do not be frightened, if you suffer for doing what is right you will be blessed.
- Be prepared to tell others why you have hope. Do it with gentleness and respect.
- Keep a clear conscience by doing what is right.
- Other:

Session 27--

1. False prophets, false teachers, distort the truth, and exploit people for their own purposes.
2.

Verses	Peter's Main Points
1-2	Stimulate wholesome thinking and remind them what the prophets had foretold.
3-4	Scoffers will doubt Jesus' return because after so many generations it has not happened.
5-6	God's creation was flooded because of sin.
8-9	God's timing may seen slow but he is patient, allowing more time for the "great commission" to be completed; that all would have a chance to be saved.
10	Before the world was destroyed with a flood. This time it will be destroyed by fire.
11-12	We need to live holy and Godly lives as we look for, anticipate the end to come.
13-14	Look forward to God's new heaven and new earth.

3. Peter came to accept the fact that Jesus died for Jews and Gentiles; for all who believe.
4. Saul
5.

Verses	Key Events of Saul
1-6	Jesus asks him why he was persecuting him.
7-9	He was blinded for three days.
10-19	Ananias healed his blindness. He was baptized and spent several days with the disciples.
20-22	He surprised everyone as he began to preach that Jesus was the Christ. He was now a converted believer.
23-25	The Jews conspired to kill him, but he escaped.
26-27	Disciples feared him but Barnabas intervened and the Apostles accepted him.
28-30	The Jews tried to kill him, but he escaped.

6. Paul
7. Christians (Only other place the name Christian is used: 1 Peter 4:16.) (Point out the cities mentioned on a map.)
8. Believers (Gentiles): Urged him, were glad, and honored the Word.
   Nonbelievers (Jews): Jealous, and abusive; kicked him out of town.

9. There was a plot to mistreat him and stone him. (Iconium was located in west-central Turkey.)

10. He was stoned and left for dead. (Lystera was also located in west-central Turkey.)

11. Paul reported all God had done through them and that they opened the door of faith to the Gentiles.

12.

Passages	Paul's Comments
1:6-7	False teachings from new Jewish converts.
3:1-5	The Holy Spirit comes because of faith, not by keeping the law.
3:10	Keeping all of the law is not possible.
3:26	We are children of God through faith in Jesus Christ.
5:3-6	We are not justified by the law, but by faith in Christ Jesus.

Session 27 Discussion Questions with Thought Starters

1. The world was destroyed with a flood because of mankind's sin. Next time it will be destroyed by fire. Should we Christians be concerned about this?
- No, we should not be overly concerned with God in control.
- We need to live holy and Godly lives so that others will see our good works and desire to have what we have: hope and assurance in the future.
- As we anticipate the end of time which is when Jesus will return; we look forward to a new heaven and earth without sin. Perfection and harmony will be the way it will be.
- According to prophecy we are told that we can see the events unfolding that will lead up to Jesus' return.
- Other:

2. God's creation was destroyed with a flood because of sin. Have we learned our lesson to not sin? Why or why not?
- No, we have not learned the lesson.
- Sin separated us from God.
- The devil roams the world seeking people to deceive and carry out his sinful plans.
- The impact of sinful mankind will continue to escalate until Jesus returns.
- Sin will cease when the devil is cast into hell forever.
- Other:

3. Saul's heavenly vision was enough to convince him Jesus was real. It was hard for all of the believers he had been trying to persecute to accept him. When we become aware of someone who is a new believer, how should we treat them?
- Befriend them.
- Make them feel welcome into the community of believers.

- Help them grow their faith.
- Involve them in the Lord's work.
- Be a Godly example.
- Other:

Session 28---

1. Paul planned to revisit the towns he visited in his first missionary journey to see how they were doing and encourage them to remain true to the faith.

2.

Verses	Key Activities
4	The decisions of the Apostles provided rules for proper worship, doctrine, and behavior for Christians. (See Acts 15:23-29 for an example.)
5	They continued with a strong emphasis on evangelism, preaching and teaching the unbelievers.

3.

Passages	Towns	Persecution
16:6-8	Phrygia, Galatia, and Troas (Turkey)	None mentioned.
16:11-12 & 22-23	Philippi	Flogged and put into prison.
17:1-5	Thessalonica	Mob and riots.
17:10-14	Berea	Stirred up crowds, had to leave
17:16-17 & 32	Athens	Sneered and disputed.
18:1, 5-6 & 17	Corinth	Abused and synagogue leader was beaten.
18:19-20	Ephesus	None mentioned.
18:22	Caesarea & Antioch	None mentioned.

4.

Passages	Paul's Main Points
3:1-7	He encouraged and strengthened them to remain faithful.
4:1-12	Urged them to live God pleasing lives.
4:13-18	Encouraged them to be hopeful and look forward to Jesus' return.
5:12-19	Encouraged proper Christian behavior.

5. False prophets will claim to be God. There will be counterfeit miracles, signs, and wonders. Stand firm to the teachings of the Word. Remain hopeful about Christ's return.

6. (A) 6. (A) Paul's main mission was to strengthen the churches, to help them learn God's truth and grow their faith.

(B)

Passages	Paul's Tactics
19:8	Preached and taught boldly and persuasively.
19:11-12	God performed miracles through him.
20:1-2	Spoke many words of encouragement.
20:18-20	Led by example, being sincere and a positive witness.

7.

Passages	Issues Paul Addresses
3:1-3	Jealousy and quarreling.
4:18-19	Arrogant people.
5:1 & 9-11	Sexual immorality.
6:1,4 & 7-8	Disputes.
7:1-40	Marriage
8:4	Eating food sacrificed to idols.
11:20-22	Lord's Supper done correctly.
13:4-8	Love
14:12	Use of spiritual gifts to build up the church.
15:3-8	Jesus's death and resurrection.
15:42-44 & 52-54	Resurrection of the dead.
16:1-2	Giving to the needy.

8.

Passages	Issues Paul Addresses
2:5-10	Forgiveness and church discipline.
5:17	With Christ we are a new creation; old behaviors are to be gone.
6:14	Do not be yoked together with unbelievers.
9:6-8	Give generously; God loves a cheerful giver.

Session 28 Discussion Questions with Thought Starters

1. The Apostles provided rules for proper worship, doctrine, and behavior for the new Christian churches. They continued with a strong emphasis on evangelism, preaching and teaching the unbelievers. Where should churches today place strong emphasis?
- Preaching the Word
- Evangelizing unbelievers
- Bible study
- Fellowship
- Growing faith
- Other:

2. Paul encouraged proper Christian behavior. What are proper Christian behaviors today?
- Prayer
- Actions speak louder than words; doing and not just saying.
- Regular worship
- Forgiving others
- Avoid gossip and slander
- Obey the laws

- Golden rule
- Other:

3. Paul said that we are not to be yoked together with unbelievers. What does this really mean?
- We can be friends with unbelievers but we need to draw a line on what we say, how we act, and what we do so that we project proper Christian attitudes, values, and behaviors.
- We need to let our light shine among unbelievers.
- Marriage to an unbeliever usually adds extra levels of stress.
- Believers and unbelievers base most beliefs and values from different points of view.
- We need to be careful we are not led astray form our faith in God.
- Other:

Session 29--

1.

Verses	Paul's Suffering
23	In prison a number of times, flogged, and exposed to death.
24	Received 39 lashes five times.
25	Beaten three times with rods, stoned, ship wrecked three times, and spent a day and night in the sea.
26	Constantly on the move, on dangerous rivers, faced bandits, and faced danger from many fronts.
27	Went without sleep, food, water, was cold, and was naked.
28	Suffered from daily pressures.

2.

Passages	Paul's Main Points
1:16	Salvation from Jesus is for Jews and Gentiles.
1:17	The righteous shall live by faith.
3:23	All have sinned and fallen short of God's glory.
3:24-25	We are justified through the redemption that came by Jesus being our sacrifice.
5:8	While we were still sinners Christ died for us.
6:23	The wages of sin is death but the gift of God is eternal life in Christ Jesus.
8:28	All things God works for the good for those who love him.
12:1-2	We are to offer our bodies as living sacrifices as we do his will.
12:4-8	We are compared to parts of a body as we work cooperatively together.
12:9-19	Love is shown by actions, not just words.

3. (A) Rome
(B) Rome

4.

Passages	Major Events
21:27-40	Paul was almost killed by a mob because they did not like his preaching and teaching about Jesus.
22:1 - 23:11	Paul defended his faith and himself. He was put into prison for his own protection.
23:12-35	Paul was taken to Caesarea to avoid the plot to kill him.
24:1-27	Paul went on trial before Felix, the governor.
25:1-12	Two years later Paul went on trial before the new governor, Festus. Paul appealed his case to Caesar.
25:13 - 26:32	Festus turned Paul's case over to King Agrippa. The King agreed that the case should go to Caesar in Rome.
27:1-28:10	Paul's journey as a prisoner to Rome experienced severe storms and a ship wreck on the island of Malta.
28:11-30	Paul finally arrived at Rome and put under house arrest. Paul continued to preach about Jesus and about the kingdom of God. Some believed and some didn't.

5.

Passages	Paul's Main Points to the Ephesians
1:4-8	Redemption from sin is through Jesus the Christ.
1:9-10	When Christ returns he will be the leader of everything.
2:8-9	We are saved through faith, not works.
2:10	We were created to do good works.
4:3-6	We are to work toward unity among all believers. There is one Lord, one faith, and one baptism; one God and Father of all.
6:10-18	To resist temptation we are to put on the full armor of God: truth, righteousness, faith, word of God, and prayer.

6.

Passages	Paul's Main Points to the Philippians
1:27-30	Paul encouraged them to stand firm through their hardships and struggles.
2:1-11	Paul encouraged unity and humility among the believers.
3:12-14	The Christian life is compared to a race and winning the prize, which is everlasting life.

7.

Verses	Paul's Main Points to the Colossians
16	Paul discusses rules pertaining to eating, drinking, and keeping religious festivals.
18	Paul warned against false humility and the worship of angels.
23	Paul warned about self inflicted pain as penance for one's sin.

8. (A) 11
(B) 10

9. Our Christ-like behaviors need to comprehend and demonstrate that race, economic status, or other differences no longer need to divide us. We are to teach and admonish each other. We are to work together to build the church. We have been given gifts to use for the work of the Lord.

10.

Verses	Questions	Answers
10	What was the slave's name?	Onesimus
15	Why was the slave with Paul?	Probably a run-away slave.

16	Why did Paul call him a brother?	He was a believer and helper to Paul.
17-18	How did Paul restore the slave's relationship with his master?	Willingly paid the price for any wrong doing.

Session 29 Discussion Questions with Thought Starters

1. How do all things God work out for the good for those who love God?
   - God has everything within his control.
   - Like a game of chess, God has 2, 3 or more moves in mind for our future and we usually cannot see how things will play out.
   - In the Lord's Prayer we pray "thy will be done on earth as it is in heaven".
   - Sometimes things will end up much different than we think it should. Provide an example from your life's experiences.
   - Other:

2. Give examples of how love is shown by actions, not just words.
   - Visit an elderly person or give them a ride to church.
   - Help a needy person or family.
   - Help your neighbor with a hard task.
   - Share your time, talents, treasures and tithes with others.
   - Explain your faith to a nonbeliever.
   - Other:

3. How are we to offer our bodies as living sacrifices as we do God's will?
   We need to do things that sometimes we would prefer not doing; for example:
   - Volunteer at a homeless shelter or a soup kitchen.
   - Teach a Bible class.
   - Help children with their school work.
   - Visit someone in prison.
   - Repair something in an elderly person's home.
   - Pray for others.
   - Other:

4. Paul taught about how believers are to treat one another. What are some of the things Christians should avoid as they let their light shine?
   - Gossip
   - Discriminating against others for any reason.
   - Not telling others about Jesus.
   - Not befriending others.
   - Other:

Session 30---

1. After Paul's two year imprisonment in Rome, he was set free. Evidence from historians suggests that he went on a fourth missionary journey that lasted for about __four__ years. Leaving from __Rome__ he traveled west to ____Spain__ . Then he traveled all the way back to __Asia__ ____Minor__ to some of the same churches he had worked with in his second and third missionary journeys. Finally, he traveled back to __Rome__ . The length of this journey was about _4000_ miles in all. It was during this journey that Paul wrote his first letter to Timothy and a letter to Titus.

2.

Passages	Paul's Main Points
1:15	Jesus came into the world to save sinners.
2:5-6	There is one God and one mediator between God and man; and that is Jesus.
3:1-13	Qualifications for church leaders are discussed.
4:9-10	We have hope for eternal life through faith in Jesus.

3.

Verses	Titus' Tasks
5	Straighten things out (organize churches) and appoint elders.
10-11	Silence the rebels with proper teaching.
13-14	Rebuke them sharply so they will be sound in their faith.
15-16	Remain pure even though they are detestable, disobedient, and unfit for doing anything good.

4.

Verses	To Who?
2	Older men
3-5	Older women and younger women
6-8	Young men
9	Slaves

5.

Verses	Two Trustworthy Points
3-6	Our Savior saved us by his grace, not by anything that we have done.
7-8	We are justified by God's grace and are heirs of the hope of eternal life.

6.

Passages	Christ is Superior to:
1:1-4	Angels
3:1-4	Moses
7:23-28	The high priests

7. Jesus died as a ransom to set all believers free from their sins and gain eternal life.

8.

Verses	Three Main Points
1	Faith is being sure of what we hope for even though we cannot see it.
6a	Without faith it is impossible to please God.
6b	God rewards those who earnestly seek him.

9.

Passages	Conditions Paul faced in the Roman Prison
1:15	Everyone had deserted him.
4:6	He understood that his death would soon come.
4:10	Demas and Crescens left him alone.
4:14	Alexander did Paul a great deal of harm.(1 Timothy 1:20)
4:16	He had no support at his court hearing.

10.

Passages	Actions
1:14	Guard the Gospel and teachings.
3:14-17	Continue in the Scriptures.
4:1-4	- Preach the Word - Correct, rebuke, and encourage with patience and careful instruction.
4:5	Endure hardships and discharge all duties of the ministry.

Session 30 Discussion Questions with Thought Starters

1. Slavery was mentioned because it was part of Roman culture. Which of the following attributes listed below apply to people today, weather you are a student, a spouse, an employee, or whatever? Slaves were to:
   a. Be subject to their master.
   b. Please their master.
   c. Not to back-talk to their master.
   d. Not steal from their master.
   e. Be trustworthy to their master

- All of these attributes are appropriate for Christians. We all have a boss.
- We all need to:
   o be respectful to those over us
   o please others
   o show respect to others
   o not steal from anyone
   o be honest
- Other:

2. The Jewish high priests were able to forgive sins, but they were sinners too. They sacrificed "spotless" animals to gain God's forgiveness. Jesus was made perfect. When he faced temptation he resisted. Jesus was always obedient to his Father. Therefore he was made perfect forever and was the perfect (spotless) sacrifice for all believers for all time. What else can we do to assure our sins are forgiven?

- There is nothing we can do for the forgiveness of our sins. Jesus paid the price once and for all.

- We need to frequently confess our sins to God and ask for forgiveness.
- We need to remain faithful to Jesus because only he provides the path to forgiveness and everlasting life.
- Other:

3. Faith is being sure of what we hope for even though we cannot see it. Without faith it is impossible to please God. How can we grow our faith?
- Faith grows from reading and studying the Bible.
- Faith grows from hearing the Word preached to us.
- Faith grows when we give our tithes we see how God provides for our needs.
- Faith grows when we see miracles happen.
- Faith grows when we experience our prayers being answered.
- Other:

4. In 1 Timothy 4-6 Paul discussed many behaviors and attitudes that are appropriate and necessary for a healthy Christian life. This letter from Paul reads like a manual for proper Christian living. What are some of the behaviors and attitudes we Christians need to live by?
- Have nothing to do with godless myths and old wives tales.
- Put our hope in the living God who is the Savior.
- We are to use our spiritual gifts.
- Stay true to proper doctrine.
- Treat people kindly.
- Put your religion into practice and care for those in need.
- Keep ourselves pure from sins.
- Be of service to others.
- Godliness with contentment is great gain.
- We are to be content with what we have.
- Love of money is the root of all kinds of evil, so avoid it.
- Pursue righteousness, godliness, faith, love, endurance, and gentleness.
- The rich are not to be arrogant or put their hope in wealth.
- Put our hope in God who richly provides everything for our enjoyment.
- Do good and be rich in good deeds.
- Be generous and willing to share.
- Other:

Session 31---

1. (A) James, Jesus's brother.
   (B) To Jews who converted to Christianity and who had scattered out among
the nations.

2.

Passages	James' Main Points
1:2-4	When our faith is tested though difficult times or grievous temptations; we persevere and grow more mature in our faith.
1:5-6	God will provide wisdom if we ask for it.
1:13-15	God does not tempt, only the devil does. If we give into temptation it can lead to eternal death.
1:19-20	We need to be quick to listen and slow to speak or get angry.
1:25	The faithful who keep God's law will find freedom and will be blessed.
1:26	We need to be careful of what we say.
1:27	Real religion involves looking after the needy, orphans, and widows. Don't let your mind be polluted by the world.
2:14-17	Faith without works is dead.
3:13-17	Realize that there are two kinds of wisdom, earthly (Devil's) and heavenly (God's).
4:17	Realize that there are sins of omission, or not doing the right thing when the opportunity presents itself.
5:7-8	We are to be patient for the Lord's return.
5:13-16	A prayer from a righteous person is powerful and effective.

3. All have sinned. It is a lie to say otherwise. But if we confess our sins to God, he
will forgive them and purify us from all unrighteousness.

4. We are not to be enticed by the sins of the world because someday the world
will be destroyed. We are to remain faithful to God and we will live forever with
him.

5. (A) antichrist
   (B)

Passages	What is He Like?
1 John 2:18	Many antichrists have already come.
1 John 2:22	They deny that Jesus is the Christ.
1 John 2:23	They do not accept Jesus as God's son.
2 John 7	They deceive people and deny Jesus the Christ came in the flesh.

6. We can test the person by what they confess and believe. If they refuse to
acknowledge Jesus as the Son of God, they are the antichrist. You can also get a
clue about a person by what they do, by their fruits.

7. John warns against allowing a false teacher or false pastor to stay in your
home. Inviting them in for conversation and witnessing would be acceptable.

8. John was thankful Gaius was being hospitable to the missionaries.

9. (A) Diotrephes' leadership in the church was abusive and overbearing.
   (B)

Examples	
He loved to be first.	Refused to welcome the brothers.

Would have nothing to do with John.	Stopped those who would welcome the brothers.
Malicious gossip.	Put people out of the church for helping the brothers

10. Want to talk about: The salvation we all share because of Jesus.

Did talk about: Urged them to remain faithful because some had allowed their faith to slip away because of godless influences they were exposed to.

11.

Verses	Examples of God's Judgment
5	He delivered his people from slavery in Egypt.
	He destroyed nonbelievers.
6	Some fallen angels who are bound in chains until judgment day.
7a	Sodom and Gomorrah were destroyed because of their sins.
7b	Future: Eternal punishment for nonbelievers in Jesus.

12.

Verses	Jude's Advice and Warnings
18	Know that there will be scoffers who will follow their own ungodly desires.
19	There will be those who will divide you.
20	Grow your faith and pray in the Spirit.
21	Remain faithful and Jesus will bring you to eternal life.
22-23	Continue to help those who lack faith or are in doubt.

Session 31 Discussion Questions with Thought Starters

1. We are not to be enticed by the sins of the world because someday the world will be destroyed. What are some of the ways the world entices people today?
- Ungodly TV programming. What is contrary to God's word is made out to be perfectly normal and okay.
- Materialism, the quest for more.
- Video games that encourage improper thinking and attitudes.
- The hype about some sports events draws people away from God; i.e. Super Bowl, Indy 500; World Series, etc.
- False pastors and teachers.
- Lyrics of popular songs.
- Other?

2. Some people accept God but not his son, Jesus. List some examples of this antichrist attitude prevalent in our world today.
- Jehovah's Witnesses claim Jesus was a son of God, not the Son of God.
- Muslims accept God but not Jesus as God's only Son.
- Mormons believe in teachings beyond what the Bible teaches.
- Other:

3. John was thankful Gaius was being hospitable to the missionaries. How can we also be hospitable to missionaries?
- When we see them offer our thanks for their work.
- Show gratitude for their efforts by helping as the needs arise.
- Financially support their work.
- Show them we care.
- Other:

4. Jude urged the believers to remain faithful because some had allowed their faith to slip away and because of godless influences. In what ways do Christians today allow their faith to slip away?
- Miss church services.
- Fail to pray daily.
- Take on activities that consume time otherwise used for doing good deeds.
- Fail to daily read and study God's Word.
- Other:

Session 32--

1. We started this Bible study in the book of _____Genesis_____ in which we saw how God created the world and everything in it. But, _sin_ entered into his perfect creation. God established a _____covenant_____ with his people to provide a path of redemption. Later, he even sent his son, _Jesus_ to be that perfect _____sacrifice_____ to redeem all people who believe from their sins. In the book of Revelation we see how God's plan of justice and salvation will be played out as all _nonbelievers_ are judged and destroyed once and for all. And, to the faithful, _____eternal_____ _life_ will be given as promised.

2. Jesus sent an angel to John.

3. They are blessed.

4. All people will see Jesus when he returns.

5. (A) Write to the seven churches in the province of Asia which today is in western Turkey.

(B) _____

Passages	Church	Good or Bad
2:1-6	Ephesus	Was good now going bad, repent or else...
2:8-11	Smyrna	Good
2:12-16	Pergamum	Was good now going bad, repent or else...
2:18-23	Thyatira	Some good and some bad.
3:1-5	Sardis	Some good but others need to repent or else....
3:8-10	Philadelphia	Good
3:14-16	Laodicea	Luke warm is not good, repent or else......

6. They will gain everlasting life.

7.

Passages	Questions	Answers
4:1	Where did the open door lead?	Heaven
4:2-3	Who did John first see?	God on his throne
4: 4	Who sat around the throne?	24 elders
4:5	Who was positioned before the throne? (See Isaiah 11:2)	Seven spirits of God (the seven aspects of the Holy Spirit)
4:6-8	Who else was positioned around the throne? (See Ezekiel 10:14 and Genesis 3:24)	Four celestial beings, most likely the Cherubim
5:6-8	Who was the only one worthy to take the scroll (God's plan for the future) from God and open it?	Jesus

8. Conditions in most aspects of peoples' lives will worsen as Satin tries to rule the earth. The frequency and intensity of undesirable conditions will increase until Jesus returns.

9. A third of mankind killed in war against a huge army of 200 million troops.

10. No remorse shown. They will continue to practice their evil ways.

11.

Verses	Actions of the Antichrist
12	Will exercised all authority, very powerful.
13	Will perform great miracles.
14	Will deceive the people on earth.
15	Will kill all who will not worship him.
16	Will force everyone to receive a mark on their right hand or forehead.
17	Will not allow anyone to buy or sell without the mark of the beast.
18	Will require his mark to be "666".

12. Jesus and the army from heaven.

13. They will be thrown into a lake of fire where they will be always in torment.

14. (A) Book of Life
   (B) A record of all of the faithful.
   (C) A record of what unbelievers had done during their lifetime.

15.

Verses	Details of God's Plan to Start Over
1	There will be a new heaven and earth, the old will pass away.
2	The new Jerusalem will come down from heaven.
3	God will dwell with mankind.
4	There will be no more death, pain, or sorrow.
5	Everything will be made new.
22	There is no temple, but God and the Lamb (Jesus) are its temple.
23	There will be no need for the sun because the glory of God gives light and Jesus is the lamp.
24	Nations and kings will bring splendor unto it.
25	The city will have no need for gates, there will be no night.
27	Nothing impure will ever enter the New Jerusalem

Session 32 Discussion Questions with Thought Starters

1. The letters to the seven churches applied to the church about 2000 years ago just as it does today. How?
- Warning to churches to be doing God's work.
- The church's mission is clear; take the gospel to the lost.
- Churches can repent and change.
- Churches need to be doers of the Word, not just hearers.
- Churches need to be sure they are preaching and teaching only the truth as found in the Bible.
- While these were letters to the seven churches, this can also be a forewarning to each individual believer to remain true to the one Christian faith and that we need to let our lights shine with good deeds.
- Other:

2. How do you know that your name is written in the "Book of Life"?
- If you can call Jesus your Lord and Savior, your name is in the Book.
- Repent of your wrongful deeds.
- Actively practice your faith with good deeds because faith without works is dead.
- Other:

3. Now that you have completed this complete Bible study, what are some options for additional Bible study?
- One Bible study needs to be viewed as just the beginning of understanding God's word.
- Study each book of the Bible in greater detail.
- Daily Bible reading.
- Teach a Bible class: youth, teens, or adults. They all need to grow in their faith. You can learn a lot by teaching.
- Other:
  - Praise God from whom all blessings flow.

Printed in the United States
By Bookmasters